Sebastian Dabovich

The Lives of the Saints, and Several Lectures and Sermons

Sebastian Dabovich

The Lives of the Saints, and Several Lectures and Sermons

ISBN/EAN: 9783337087746

Printed in Europe, USA, Canada, Australia, Japan

Cover: Foto ©Lupo / pixelio.de

More available books at **www.hansebooks.com**

THE LIVES OF THE SAINTS

AND SEVERAL LECTURES AND SERMONS

COMPILED AND TRANSLATED BY

REV. SEBASTIAN DABOVICH

FOR DEVOTIONAL FAMILY READING
AND SCHOOL PRACTICE

These Readings have been delivered
before the Congregation
in the Presence of the
Most Reverend Bishop Nicholas

SAN FRANCISCO
The Murdock Press
1898

COPYRIGHT, 1898,
BY
SEBASTIAN DABOVICH

DEDICATED TO THE SACRED MEMORY OF

ISIDORUS,

Who served the Church of God for sixty-seven years; *Who* presided in the Most Holy Synod of the Russian Orthodox Church for thirty-two years; *Who* was the most faithful friend, spiritual adviser, and material support, under God, of the young Church in North America in her many serious trials, temptations, and persecutions; *Who*, in the midst of Episcopal Ordinaries, was the Chief Consecrator of all the Bishops of the Orthodox American Church down to the present worthy Successor of the first great Missionary and Bishop of Alaska, and *Who*, steadfast in the work of his Master to the very last, peacefully commended his soul to God, (having completed his ninety-third year,) on the 7-19 of September, 1892 — by the

TRANSLATOR AND AUTHOR,

who had the good fortune of obtaining his first official appointment to service in the ranks of the Clergy from the *Most Reverend Isidorus, Metropolitan of Novgorod, St. Petersburg, and Finland,* and who furthermore had the spiritual consolation and privilege to obtain his personal blessing and to kiss the hand of the greatest *Prelate* of the day.

PREFACE.

In this, our second book, we cheerfully offer to our brethren and children of the Holy Orthodox Church in the English-speaking world the Lives of the Saints, together with some lectures and a few of our sermons,—mindful of the command of our Master, who said: *Freely ye have received, freely give.* We have no comments to make; let the facts in the histories of the lives of holy men and women speak for themselves; we only repeat that, *the Spirit breatheth where He will.* Let our lectures and sermons likewise speak for themselves, as they are strictly founded upon Holy Scripture and the writings of the Holy Fathers of the Church in her early days.

HIEROMONACHOS SEBASTIAN.

SAN FRANCISCO, September 14-26, 1898.

CONTENTS.

	PAGE
ST. JOHN THE BAPTIST	9
ST. MARY MAGDALENE	17
ST. JOHN THE EVANGELIST	22
ST. PANTELEIMON, THE GREAT MARTYR	30
ST. NICHOLAS, ARCHBISHOP OF MYRA IN LYCIA	46
ST. NINA, THE MISSIONARY OF GEORGIA	57
A SAINTED BROTHER'S HISTORY OF A SAINTED SISTER	68
ST. JOHN CHRYSOSTOM	77
SOMETHING ABOUT AN EVENING HYMN	84
ST. PELAGIA	92
STS. CYRIL AND METHODIUS, THE APOSTLES OF THE SLAVONIANS	99
ST. SABBAS, THE FIRST ARCHBISHOP OF THE SERVIANS	120
ST. ALEXANDER NEVSKY	123
ST. PHILIP, METROPOLITAN OF MOSCOW	135
WHY CHRISTIANS BRING LOAVES TO THE DIVINE LITURGY	152

CONTENTS.

	PAGE
Address at the Celebration of the One Hundredth Anniversary of the Great Missionary in North America	164
Sincere Religion	174
Sermon on Orthodox Sunday	184
Sermon for the Fifth Sunday After Trinity	192
Sermon on Twentieth Sunday After Trinity	198
How the Church Cares for Her Sheep and Lambs	209

Beloved, while I was giving all diligence to write unto you of our common salvation, I was constrained to write unto you exhorting you to contend earnestly for the faith which was once for all delivered unto the saints. (Jude, 3.)

THE LIFE OF ST. JOHN THE BAPTIST.

SAINT JOHN THE BAPTIST was the son of the Jewish Priest Zacharia. His mother was Elizabeth, a blood-relation to the Most Blessed Virgin Mary. This righteous couple were childless, for Elizabeth was barren. They prayed much and long; as true Israelites they desired the consolation of being blessed with children, aspiring,— but in this instance with an humble and holy resignation — to the birth of the great Messiah, who was coming to save mankind, and, as they thought, to free and unite Israel. Although Zacharia and Elizabeth sorrowed in their old age to a day which was beyond the natural limit of child-bearing, still they continued hopefully praying. The prayers of faith of this priest and his patient spouse ascended on high, from whence came down an angel with the message telling them that the Creator of nature and the God of wonders had been pleased to fulfill their desire.

Accordingly, Elizabeth bore unto her husband Zacharia a male child, who was called John.

This John was called by God to be the forerunner of his Divine Son, to usher Him into the world, and to prepare mankind by repentance to receive the Redeemer, whom the prophets had foretold at a distance through every age from the beginning of the world, never ceasing to instill in the people of God faith and hope in Him by whom alone they were to be saved. At first St. John led a most austere life in the wilderness, exercising himself in prayer and meditating on the high mission he was called to perform. In the thirtieth year of his age, John came from out his seclusion. This was also the age at which the priests and Levites were permitted by the Jewish law to begin the exercise of their functions. Clothed in camel's hair, held to his person by a girdle of raw leather, the man of the desert, who knew not the luxuries of a dwelling-house, nor the taste of cooked food, himself subsisting on locusts and wild honey, comes to the thinly settled banks of the river Jordan, and preaches repentance, baptizing all comers. *Make ye the way straight,* says he; *for cometh He whose sandal-strap I am not worthy to unloose; He shall baptize you with the Holy Ghost and with fire.* John was received by the people as the true herald of the Most High God. All classes of people came and listened to him. Among them were many Pharisees, whose pride and hypocrisy, which rendered them indocile and blinded them in their vices, he sharply reproved. The very soldiers and publicans, or tax-collectors, who were generally persons hardened in habits of immorality, violence, and injustice, flocked to him. He exhorted all to works of charity and to a reformation of their lives, and those who addressed themselves to him in these dispositions, he baptized in the river.

The baptism of John differed entirely from the great Christian sacrament of baptism, as the first was an emblem of the effects of living in the fear of the justice of God by abstaining from evil deeds, whilst the latter wholly delivers us from the original sin and the consequences, and makes us the children of God, by the grace of our Lord Jesus Christ.

When St. John had already preached and baptized about six months, the Lord Jesus went from Nazareth, and presented Himself, among others, to be baptized by him. The Baptist knew Him by a divine revelation, and, full of awe and respect for his sacred person, at first excused himself, but at length acquiesced out of obedience. The Saviour of sinners was pleased to be baptized among sinners, not to be cleansed Himself, but to sanctify the waters, and to manifest Himself to the world, which was represented in the great mass of people which came to John. *And John bear witness of Him.* Pointing Him out before the Jews, John said, *Behold the Lamb of God, which taketh away the sin of the world!* John the Baptist reproved the vices of all men, no matter who they were, with an impartial freedom and in a fearless spirit. He disclosed the hypocrisy of the Pharisees, and uncovered the profaneness of the Sadducees; he denounced the fraud of certain government officials,—*i. e.* the publicans,— the rapine and licentiousness of the soldiers, and the incest of King Herod himself. Now, Herod had unlawfully taken unto himself Herodias, the wife of his own brother Philip, who was still living. When the saint said to the king, *It is not lawful for thee to have her,*

Herodias set herself against him, and desired to kill John. Herod reverenced John as a holy man; therefore he dared not harm him. Nevertheless he had the saint within his reach, in prison, for he could not bear to have the sore spot of his weak conscience tampered with. St. John faithfully completed his mission, and he understood when his time was up; even before this, he said, *Jesus must increase, but I must decrease.* While in confinement the righteous preacher was still anxious to bear testimony to the glory of the Saviour; we read furthermore in the Gospel that, on hearing in prison of Christ's wonderful works and preaching, John sent two of his disciples to Him for their information, not doubting but that Christ would satisfy them that He was the Messiah; and that by His answers they would lay aside their prejudices, and join themselves to Him.

Herod continued to respect John; he would sometimes send for him, and listen to him with pleasure, though he was troubled when he was admonished by him for his faults. In the mean time Herodias sought an opportunity to compass the Baptist's destruction. An occasion at length fell out favorable to her designs. It was on the birthday anniversary of the king, when he made in his castle a splendid entertainment for the nobility of Galilee. During a sumptuous repast, Salome, a daughter of Herodias by her lawful husband, danced before the guests, and so pleased the king by her dancing, that he promised her, with the sacred bond of an oath, to grant her whatever she asked, though it amounted to half of his dominions. The damsel consulted with her mother, and she dispatched her daughter with haste, to demand that the head of John the Baptist be brought in to her at once on a charger. This strange request startled the drunken tyrant himself. He, however, assented, though with reluctance, *but for the sake of his oaths, and of them that sat at meat,* he ordered a soldier of his guard to strike off the head of St. John. In this way the bloody head of the holy prophet was brought into the hall, where they ate and drank and made merry with music, and it was given to the young dancer, who took it and carried it to her mother. No doubt Herod had no thought of the oath, while giving it, that it was a sinful one, but he committed a much greater sin by keeping his oath. And thus it was that John the Baptist, the man of the desert, ended his life, one of the chief causes of his death being a sinful supper. But, by God's mercy, he was not put to death before he had fulfilled his great duty as the forerunner of our Lord Jesus Christ. The many virtues of St. John, those of a martyr, a virgin, a teacher, and a prophet, were exalted in praise by Christ Himself, when he said to the multitudes of the people: *Verily, I say unto you, there hath not risen among them that are born of women a greater than John the Baptist. When his disciples hearing that John was executed in prison, they came and took his body and laid it in a tomb.*

The misfortunes which befell Herod after the death of John the Baptist, the Jews said were punishments from God for the murder of his servant, as their historian, Joseph Flavius, records. Aretas, the King of Arabia, and the father of Herod's first wife, struck a deadly blow at the army of the Galilean ruler. Soon after this the Roman emperor banished Herod into exile. The holy relics of St. John did not remain for all time in their tomb at

Sebastia. When the holy apostle Luke visited this city, he took the right arm of the saint and brought it to Antioch, where the Christians treasured it for a long time. When, in 956, the Mohammedans took possession of Antioch, a deacon by the name of Job carried the relic to Halcedon, from which place it was brought, on the eve of the Epiphany, to Constantinople. The Turkish sultan, Bajazet, desiring to please the Crusaders, presented the Knights of Malta with the arm of the great Baptist. In 1799, this order of knights sent the relic of St. John to the Emperor Paul I. of Russia, and the great prophet's arm may be seen to this day in the royal palace in the "Chapel of the Saviour's Uncreated Image." The Holy Church celebrates the birth of St. John the Baptist on the 24th of June. On the 29th of August, she commemorates his beheading. And on the 7th of January, the Church praises the great saint for his whole life, his works, and his mission, as he was selected to be the baptizer of Jesus Christ, the Son of God.

ST. MARY MAGDALENE, THE CO-EQUAL WITH THE APOSTLES.

July 22.

ONCE when the Lord Jesus Christ went about Galilee creating miracles and signs by His divine power, a woman who was known by the name of Mary Magdalene approached Him and implored for His mercy. The Lord cast out from her seven demons, and liberated her entirely from the disease with which she suffered. From this time on the grateful Mary served the Lord, heard His teaching, and followed Him even to the cross-death. Together with other holy women, she looked upon the sufferings of Christ, and wept for Him. She, in company with the Mother of our Lord, stood by the cross, and beheld where they laid His body in the tomb.

The holy women, overwhelmed with grief at the death of the Lord, prepared a sweet-smelling myrrh in order to anoint the body of Jesus Christ, as was the custom with the Jews at the burial of their dead; and after the Sabbath was past, early in the morning, they came to His grave; but before the others, yet before it was daylight, Mary Magdalene came, and, to her surprise, she found that the stone had been rolled away, and the tomb was empty. She hurriedly ran to John and Peter and said to them: *They have taken the Lord from out the tomb, and I do not know where they have put Him.* John and Peter immediately followed her, and on entering the tomb, saw that the body of Jesus was not in it, but in a corner lay the linen cloth in which the body was enveloped. At that they went away; but not Mary — she remained by the grave, and stood weeping. On stooping and looking into the tomb, she suddenly saw two angels in shining white apparel, sitting, one at the head and the other at the feet, where the body of Jesus had lain.

They said to her, *Woman, wherefor weepest thou? They have taken away my Lord,* answered she, *and I do not know where they have put Him.* As she spoke thus, she turned backward again and saw Jesus Himself standing there; but as the hour was early she did not know Him and she thought that He was the keeper of the garden.

Woman, said He to her, *why weepest thou, and who is it thou seekest?* *If thou hast taken Him,* said she, *do tell me where hast thou laid Him.* The Lord then called her by name. *Mary,* said He. On hearing His voice, she knew Him, and cried joyfully, *Rabboni.* In the Hebrew language this means "my teacher." *Touch me not,* saith Jesus, *but go unto My brethren, and say to them I ascend unto My Father and your Father, and My God and your God.* In the mean time other women came to the tomb; Mary Magdalene returned with them also. They all had seen two angels, who said to them: *Why seek ye the living among the dead? He is not here; He is risen! Go and tell His disciples and Peter that He is risen from the dead.* Filled with joy and fear, the myrrh-bearing women went from the place, and on their way they, on a sudden, met with Christ Himself, who said to them: *All hail!* They fell upon the ground and worshiped before Him.

In this way, the holy women, who served the Lord so generously during His earthly life, were counted worthy to become the first heralds — proclaiming His glorious resurrection. Mary Magdalene, the first one to see the resurrected Lord, consoled the grief-stricken disciples with these joyful words: *Christ is risen!* As the first bearer of the glad tidings of the resurrection, she has been honored by the Church with a name synonymous with "co-equal with the Apostles." After the ascension of the Lord, St. Mary continued in prayer together with the Most Holy Mother of God and the Apostles, and she was a witness of the first fruits of the Christian teaching in Jerusalem. Her great faith was manifest in the lively zeal with which she preached the Word of God, visiting different countries. Church tradition tells us, that she also came to Rome, and here she presented the Emperor Tiberius with an egg, which was colored red, while saying to him, "Christ is risen!" After this she told the emperor of the crucifixion of Christ the Lord, and accused Pilate of the unjust death-sentence which he pronounced against Jesus, the innocent Jesus. From olden days it was a custom, still kept by the Jews, especially by the poor people, to present their friends, acquaintances, and protectors on the anniversary of their birth and on New Year's Day with red eggs. They were received as an expression of joy and the show of respect on the part of those people who were not able to offer a more precious gift. Since the time of this offer of St. Mary Magdalene, it has become a custom with Christians to present one another eggs which are colored red, in remembrance of the resurrection of Christ. From Rome St. Mary, the co-equal with the Apostles, went to Ephesus, where she assisted St. John the Divine until her death. In the fifth century her holy remains were transferred from Ephesus to Constantinople.

THE LIFE OF ST. JOHN THE EVANGELIST.

ONCE, when our Lord Jesus Christ walked by the shores of the sea of Tiberias, He saw two brothers, James and John, who, with their father, Zebedee, were mending nets; for they were fishermen. He called them, and they leaving all, immediately went after Him. The Lord foretold that they would possess special zeal for His law, by naming them the sons of thunder — "Boanerges." From that time they did not leave Him. They, together with Peter, were present at the raising of the dead daughter of Jairus; they were with the Lord at the time of His transfiguration on Mount Tabor; previous to the passions of the Lord they were with Him in the garden of Gethsemane. Jesus Christ loved John especially. During the mystic supper John occupied a place near Him, and when Jesus mentioned that one of His disciples shall betray

Him, John leaned upon His breast and asked to be told of whom He spoke. Finally, when the Lord Jesus saw the most pure Virgin Mary and the beloved disciple stand by His cross before His death, He recommended one to the other by saying to His dear mother, *Behold thy son;* then to John He said, *Behold thy mother.* John took the Most Holy Mother of God to his home, and from that time served her as his own mother — up to the time of her holy assumption.

After the ascension of the Lord, John lived together with the Apostles in Jerusalem, prayed in the temple, and received the gracious gift of the Holy Ghost and the understanding of languages. Henceforth he earnestly preached the Gospel and converted both Jews and Gentiles, notwithstanding the constant persecutions he underwent for the same. After the Blessed and Ever-Virgin Mary was taken unto Her Son and God, John — in company with his disciple Prochoros — went into Asia Minor. The ship on which they took passage was wrecked. But John and Prochoros were miraculously spared, and so they came to Ephesus. But here, being without means they hired themselves as servants in the house of a certain land-owner. The master and his house-people were pagans. And the servants were obliged to labor hard, and to put up with much, while no mercy was shown to them. The apostle and his fellow worker bore all with patience. It happened that in the same house a young man died, who was the son of one of the city rulers, and the boy's father, Dioscoridus, stricken with grief at his loss, quite suddenly died himself of a broken heart. The whole community became troubled. But it was in this instance that God showed His favor to His servants. John prayed, and God returned Dioscoridus and his son to life. All became stricken with fear, and they looked upon John as upon a divine being. But the preacher of the Gospel explained to them, that it was done by God's power, and that he was sent to them to tell them of God's Son, Jesus Christ, who had revealed Himself and come to save mankind. They listened with much attention, and took the apostle and his attendant into their good keeping. In this way the Church of Ephesus had its birth. And the Word spread and became confirmed in that country. St. John continued to teach, but his words were not as effective as was his life, by which he showed what a Christian should be. The change of religion by so many people in a city like Ephesus could not escape the notice of the emperor of Rome, who at that time was Domitian. The disciple of Jesus Christ suffered much from the tyrant. But when John remained whole after being thrown into a vessel of boiling oil, the emperor gave up the task of killing him, and ordered that the apostle be exiled to the island named Patmos.

Here St. John lived and worked for several years. He was not successful immediately, but the Lord Jesus finally rewarded him for his patience. The inhabitants of Patmos gradually came to Christ by John, and this was the cause of much trouble to the preacher on the part of jealous leaders in the religion of idols. Yet the apostle persevered, and also subdued these foes by prayer and love.

After the death of Domitian, Emperor Nerva came to the throne of Rome. This was a good man, for he did not take delight in the suffering of his fellow-beings. Now John was free to go withersoever he desired. He decided to return to Ephesus. On hearing this, the whole population of the island were grieved, for they loved their teacher. To console them he promised to write for them the Gospel of Jesus Christ. He therefore ordered them to pray and fast, while he took himself with his assistant up into a mountain. He remained in prayer and fasting for three days, when suddenly the earth quaked, and a violent thunder-storm seemed to disturb all the heavens. Prochoros fell on his face in fear, but the elder took him by the arm and told him to sit and write down what he dictated. John lifted his eyes to heaven, and being inspired with the Holy Ghost, he commenced the Gospel with these words: *In the beginning was the Word, and the Word was with God, and the Word was God.* Thus was written the Gospel of St. John. For the high theology for which this Gospel is especially noted, its writer was surnamed "the Divine." It was also on Patmos that John put in writing the revelations given him from heaven. The Book of Revelations in a mystical way tells of the destination of mankind and of the terrible last judgment. The Gospel of St. John is supposed to have been written in A. D. 102.

On the return of St. John to Ephesus the Christians of all Asia Minor were made very happy. By this time the venerable apostle was an old man. Still he took delight in going all over the country, through cities and villages, comforting the faithful, and strengthening the new converts. In one of the cities of Asia Minor St. John selected a certain young man, whom he desired to take into his special guidance. The favored young man was carefully taught while the apostle abode in that place; but when he was obliged to go farther on his mission, St. John delivered him to the care of the bishop of the city. On another occasion this messenger of Jesus Christ happened to visit this city again. When St. John inquired of the bishop about his charge, and he had lost the young man given him, it was a sad story to be told. The young man having made the acquaintance of bad associates, wandered off with them to the mountains, and became himself the captain of a band of robbers. Notwithstanding his old age, the apostle went himself to the mountains to seek the bandits. The chief on seeing his men lead an old man toward himself, recognized the apostle and the disciple of love. This meeting was too much for his reproaching conscience. He turned to run; but the white-haired apostle followed him as best he could, calling out in a pitiful voice, "Come, my son, my son, come back to your father; I will take your sins upon myself; the merciful Lord had sent me Himself." The young man was taken with emotion; he stopped, but dared not look up; he fell at the feet of the saint. John kissed him as a loving father, and brought him back rejoicing, as does a shepherd who had found his lost sheep.

St. John lived more than a hundred years. He died quietly, being surrounded with the love of many faithful ones. After him, his beloved disciple Prochoros became the chief pastor of the Christians in Asia Minor. This apostle's memory is kept by the Church on two days in the year, namely, the 8th of May and the 26th of September. Besides the two books mentioned before, there are also three general epistles which belong to St. John the

Divine. During his last days upon earth, when he was too weak to do much service, he continually kept saying, *My little children, love ye one another.* In the epistles of St. John we find these passages: *He that saith I know the Lord, and keepeth not His commandments, is a liar, and the truth is not in him; but whosoever keepeth His word, in him verily hath the love of God been perfected* . . . *Whosoever hath the goods of this world, and beholdeth his brother in need, and shutteth up his compassion from him, how doth the love of God abide in him?* . . . *Herein was the love of God manifested in us, that God hath sent His only begotten Son into the world that we might live through Him.**

* The words in italics throughout the book are taken from the Holy Bible.

ST. PANTELEIMON, THE GREAT MARTYR AND UNMERCENARY PHYSICIAN.

July 27.

SAINT PANTELEIMON, the Great Martyr, was born in the city of Nicomedia, during the third century; at his birth he was given the name of *Pantoleon*, which signifies, *in all things a lion*. But as we shall see after in his life he was given the name *Panteleimon* which signifies, *all-merciful*. We shall call him by this last name. The name itself already explains for us — telling by what virtues especially the holy martyr had become celebrated. And in reality the Church praises St. Panteleimon as a healer who never took pay; a most kind physician of both bodily and spiritual ills.

Panteleimon's mother was a Christian, but she died while he was yet very young. His father, being a pagan who worshiped the

Roman idols, educated his child in the same false customs and religion. Eustorgius, the father, gave his son Panteleimon to one Euphrosinius, who was a renowned physician, that he might teach the boy the science of medicine. The new pupil of this learned master showed himself clever and at the same time industrious, with a quiet disposition. The great doctor became attached to him, and he always had the boy with him. As he was the medical adviser of the emperor, Panteleimon went with him to the palace, and the Emperor Maksimian also took a liking to the bright lad.

Panteleimon visited his teacher every day. His path lay by the humble dwelling of an old man, whose name was Ermolaus. This old Ermolaus was a Christian priest. There were other Christians also who lived with him, concealing themselves from the unbelievers, for at that time the Christians were persecuted, and the Bishop of Nicomedia, Anthemus, was put to death a little before this. The aged saint loved Panteleimon, and the Lord filled his heart with a desire to enlighten the youth with the light of the true faith. Once he invited the lad to enter his house, and here Ermolaus opened a conversation with him. He commenced by inquiring of the youth who his parents were, which religion was theirs, and what their occupation was. Panteleimon readily answered these questions of the good old man. "My mother was a Christian," said he, "and she served one God; she is now dead; my father belongs to the religion of the Hellenes, and he worships many gods." On perceiving that the open-hearted youth was anxious about the truth, and inquired for explanations, the presbyter at once spoke of the beautiful order of the universe, of the great and wise and good Creator. Then in brief he reviewed the history of mankind; of its fall, its corruption, and the different false ideas of religion. He told him of the coming into the world of the Son of God — as a man like unto ourselves, sins excepted, that He might by His teaching, His goodness, and His death, open unto us again the happiness of Paradise, and return us to our God. The words of the old man reminded Panteleimon of the first teaching of his good mother, who thus also spoke to him of the Lord when he was a little child. He listened with care, and so loved these instructions that he came every day to visit the presbyter, after leaving his medical lessons. The holy man continued to explain for him the commandments of Jesus Christ, and the heart of Panteleimon became inflamed with love to God. The Lord in His mercy strengthened his faith by a wonderful event.

It happened that, when he was once returning from his master, Panteleimon saw a little child lying dead upon the road. The cause of the death of the child was lying there next to its body — a live venomous serpent. At first the youth was frightened. But he suddenly remembered what the old man had told him of the might and goodness of God. He commenced to pray to the Lord Jesus Christ, calling upon His holy name and all-powerful assistance, when, to the delight of his pure heart, he saw the child awake as if from a deep sleep. This miracle completed the first instructions of the presbyter; for Panteleimon believed from the depth of his soul, and rejoicing and praising the Lord, he hurried to meet Ermolaus, to tell him all and to beg him for his baptism without delay.

Having become a Christian, Panteleimon

prayed God that his father also might be made to understand the truth, as he loved his father and sorrowed because he still remained a pagan. The youth often tried to convince him that his gods were false and had no power whatever; Eustorgius heard him and began to waver in his religion of many deities; finally the merciful Lord opened his understanding by divine grace. In course of time Panteleimon had become a celebrated physician, and many sick people appealed to him for relief. Once a blind man was brought to him, who said that all the healers in the city had doctored him in turn, but in vain. "I only wasted my wealth upon them," said the unfortunate man; "but I will cheerfully give you what I have left to me, if you will but cure me."

Moved by the Spirit of God, Panteleimon said to the blind man: "The Father of Light, the true God, will heal you by me, His unworthy servant; all that which you have promised me, distribute among the poor."

On hearing this conversation, his father, Eustorgius, complained: "My son, do not undertake to do that of which thou art incapable," said he. "Hearest thou not, that no physician was able to restore him his sight? how canst thou hope to succeed in this?"

"Those physicians could not cure him," answered Panteleimon; "but there is a great difference between their teachers and my teacher."

Eustorgius thought that his son spoke about the celebrated doctor, Euphrosinus, upon which he replied: "I have heard, my son, that your master, Euphrosinus, attempted to cure this blind one, but without success."

"You will now see the power of my healing, father," said Panteleimon.

He approached the blind man, and touching his eyes, said: "In the name of my Lord Jesus Christ, I say to thee, receive thy sight." And in the same instant the eyes of the blind were opened, and he could see. Greatly wondering at the exhibit of such power and the grace of God, both Eustorgius and the formerly blind man believed in the Lord. When, soon after this, Panteleimon acquainted them with Ermolaus, the old priest instructed them in the Christian law, and baptized them in the name of the Most Holy Trinity.

It was not long before the father of our

youthful saint had died, leaving him a rich inheritance. Panteleimon immediately liberated all his servants and slaves, rewarding them abundantly, and then he commenced to distribute his wealth among the needy. He visited on each day those who were confined in bonds, the sick, the unfortunate, and he succored them. The Lord gifted him with power to heal all diseases with His name; not one stricken with misery had left him without obtaining relief or assistance; the sick flocked to him in multitudes, and all the people praised the talented and unmercenary physician. This fact aroused the jealousy of all the medical men. Once some of them met upon the way the blind man whom they could not cure. They were surprised to see him in possession of his sight; they questioned him to learn who had cured him. When he told them that it was Panteleimon, they retorted: "It is no wonder, for he is the great pupil of the great master, the celebrated physician, Euphrosinus." But, loudly applauding him, they secretly hated Panteleimon, and endeavored to seek a means by which to injure him.

Continually watching his actions, they discovered that he often visits the prisons, in which at that time many Christians were confined; that he heals their infirmities and offers them money, and that he believes in Christ himself. His enemies lost no time in accusing him before the Emperor Maksimian. "Sire," said they to him, "the young man who was by your order educated in the art of healing, now abuses your kindness by using his abilities to a disgraceful advantage. He often visits the enemies of our gods, he helps them; and he himself believes in one Christ, and offers to Him the glory of his cures. If thou dost not take some measures against him, he will do much evil, and lead many astray from the true religion." At the same time, to uphold their complaint, they brought before the emperor the blind man who had been healed by Panteleimon.

"Tell me," inquired of him the ruler, "how was it that Panteleimon restored to thee thy sight?"

"He touched my eyes, and called upon the name of Jesus Christ, and I began to see," answered he who was blind.

"Thinkest thou that it was Jesus Christ who

healed thee, or our gods?" asked the ruler.

"Many physicians endeavored to cure me, and they invoked the aid of Esculapus, but I received no benefit whatever from them. When Panteleimon called the name of Christ, only then was it that I could see. And now, sire, thou mayst decide thyself which was it that cured me." The emperor found no words for reproach to this reply: however, he began to advise him who was blind to worship the gods. But he with all his heart believed in the Lord, and no advice nor command, not even persecution, could compel him to renounce himself of the Lord Jesus Christ, who healed him. At last the emperor, filled with anger, condemned him to die. After the execution Panteleimon bought of the soldiers the body of this firm confessor of his faith, and gave it a Christian burial.

Panteleimon hardly had time enough to put away the dead, when a summons came that he should appear before the emperor. He, of course, correctly surmised why he was sent for; but persecution and death for the name of Christ frightened him not, and he calmly and joyfully went before the sovereign. Maksimian concealed his anger, and received him apparently with kindness. "What is it I hear of thee, Panteleimon? It is said that thou despisest the gods and dost offer praise to some Christ, who died the death of a criminal. Can it be possible that thou hast forgotten all my attention and kindness, and hast become my enemy? No, I can not believe this, and hope that thou wilt thyself disarm thy accusers, and before all offer a sacrifice to our great gods."

"Sire, believe what they have told you of me," fearlessly answered the young man. "I in truth did renounce your false gods, and I offer glory to Christ, for according to His works I have become convinced that He is the true God. He created the universe. He raises the dead. He restores sight to the blind; to the infirm He gives strength and health." Panteleimon desired to prove for the emperor that his false gods were nothing, he therefore recommended to have an extremely sick one brought in, and that the priests of the pagan temples should be invited to pray for the return of his health. All was done as he desired. The ministers of the gods prayed to their idols in vain. But when Panteleimon called upon the sick one the name of the Lord Jesus Christ, he was healed at that instant. Many of those who witnessed such a wonder, believed in the Lord; but grace had no access to the heart of Maksimian. The idolatrous priests said to the emperor: "If Panteleimon remain alive, he will deceive many, and we will be made a laughing-stock for the Christians; we therefore demand, sire, that you give the order to seize him." The emperor requested St. Panteleimon to bend the knee before the gods, at the same time warning him of the terrible tortures for his refusal; he also reminded him of the death to which the aged Anthemus was condemned.

"If Anthemus, an old man, could bear suffering with such fortitude, then I should be the one to fear the least, young and strong as I am. To die for Christ would be for me a blessing."

Hearing these remarks of the young Christian, the emperor ordered his servants to torture him, which they did by tearing his body with sharp instruments, and then burning the sores with a torch. Panteleimon prayed: "Lord Jesus Christ," said he, "be Thou near to me, and give me patience, that I may bear this torture to the end." The Lord heard his prayer and revealed His person to him, strengthening and cheering him in the midst of suffering. Although the persecutor's wrath was horrible, yet it was feeble; in vain he sought out the most terrible tortures; he ordered the saint to be thrown into a vessel filled with melted lead; the martyr remained alive and whole. Ascribing this to the art of a sorcerer, Maksimian commanded that the Christian have a large stone tied to his neck and then be cast into the sea. But it was the Lord's pleasure to manifest in Panteleimon His power and goodness; the martyr remained alive and whole, preserved from danger by the almighty hand of God.

The emperor resolved to rid himself of Panteleimon by giving him as food to the wild beasts. The theater was prepared at the outskirts of the city; on an appointed day all the people gathered to see how the wild beasts would tear the body of the young Christian; the ruler himself arrived on the scene, and pointing to the hungry, fierce beasts, said to Panteleimon: "Save thy youthful life, and offer a sacrifice to the gods." But the Christian would rather die than renounce the Lord. The ferocious animals were let out at him; again the Lord rescued him, as He rescued Daniel of old; it seemed as though the jaws of the beasts were guarded when they came around Panteleimon, as so many meek lambs. At this many voices in the multitude called out: "Great is the God of Christians." All this only increased the anger of Maksimian. Those who dared to praise Christ he put to death. But for Panteleimon he invented new tortures. He ordered the saint tied to a wheel covered with sharp spikes; again God revealed His mercy, even to Maksimian, by showing His greatness in preserving Panteleimon in this terrible trial.

"Who has taught you to be a sorcerer?" asked the infuriated emperor.

"It is not magics, but in Christian piety, I have been taught by the priest, Ermolaus," replied the holy martyr. Panteleimon knew well that Ermolaus feared not to die for the name of Christ, so therefore he did not conceal his teacher's name.

The emperor sent Panteleimon himself to

bring Ermolaus before him. "Thou hast come for good, my son," said the aged saint, when the young man entered his house; "the time has come for me to suffer and to die for the Lord, for I have this very night seen the Lord, who told me of it. Let us go."

On coming into the presence of the emperor, Ermolaus without fear declared that he was a Christian. When questioned if he had any more associates, he named two, Ermina and Ermocrata, who lived in the same house with him. These also were summoned before the court.

"You have turned Panteleimon away from our gods?" said the emperor to the Christians.

"Christ, the God Himself, calls those whom He finds worthy," answered they.

"Endeavor to convert Panteleimon to our gods once more," said the ruler, "and then the first fault will not only be forgiven you, but you will receive a reward from me."

"We cannot do this. We would rather die for the name of our God," with firmness replied the Christians. Thereupon they began to pray, and the Lord revealed Himself to them, so that they were strengthened for that which awaited them. Suddenly a shock of earthquake was felt, soon after which it was reported to the emperor that the idols in the temple fell from their places. Not perceiving in this the almighty hand of the great Creator, Maksimian exclaimed: "If I do not put to death these sorcerers, the whole city will be destroyed!" He then commanded that Panteleimon be taken to prison, and Ermolaus, Ermina, and Ermocrata to be flogged and then beheaded. The Church keeps the memory of these three martyrs on the 26th of July.

Not being able to deceive Panteleimon, either by bribes or threats, the emperor, at last baffled in his design, ordered the martyr to be heavily flogged, and then killed at the block. The saint went to his death joyfully, chanting the Psalms of David. When they had come to the place of execution, he was tied to an olive-tree. A soldier let the blade down, but no harm came to the holy martyr, who had not yet finished his prayer. Seeing this, the guard that was there became terrified, and fell at the feet of St. Panteleimon, exclaiming: "Great is the God of Christians!" The soldiers beseeched the martyr to forgive and to pray for them. At this there came a voice from heaven, which named the martyr *Panteleimon,* instead of his former name, Pantoleon. Having prayed, the saint requested the soldiers to carry out their bidding. Finally St. Panteleimon was beheaded. The olive-tree to which he was tied was filled with fruit. Many bystanders became believers. The emperor commanded that the olive-tree be cut down, and that the body of St. Panteleimon be burned. In this instance, another miracle again proved that Panteleimon was God's faithful servant — his body was not burned in the fire. Christians took the body and buried it honorably; at the same time they made a record of the life, suffering, and death of the great martyr, and sent it, for their edification and his memory, to the holy churches. This took place A. D. 296.

At the present day, there is a part of the relics of St. Panteleimon in a monastery on Mount Athos, which is called St. Panteleimon's monastery. From olden times this convent was inhabited mostly by Russian monks, although there always have been also brethren of different nationalities.

THE LIFE OF SAINT NICHOLAS.

DURING the first ages of the Christian era, the Church suffered much persecution from wicked persons and pagan governments. To spread the faith of Christ, as well as to uphold the struggling Church, it pleased God to send into the field specially chosen men, His servants, tried in the faith, and powerful both in life and in the Word. Such, among others, was Saint Nicholas, whose memory we celebrate on the 9th of May, the occasion on which his incorruptible relics were carried from the city of Myra to the city of Bari, and also on the 6th of December, the day of his burial.

St. Nicholas was born in the second half of the third century, in the city of Patara, of the country of Lycia. From early childhood the beginnings of those virtues by which he afterwards was glorified by God before all the people, could be seen in his person and behavior. After his studies at home, having attained the age of manhood, his uncle, whose name was also Nicholas—he being the bishop of Patara—raised him to the dignity of a presbyter. During the sacrament of the laying on of hands, the bishop, being inspired with a spirit of prophecy, turned to the congregation, and showing the young man, exclaimed: "Brethren, I see a new sun, rising above the earth, and promising comfort to all the suffering. Blessed is the flock which shall have him for its pastor; for he will bring the wandering sheep to the truth, he will pasture them in the meadows of piety, and be a helper to all which sorrow." The whole life of St. Nicholas was a fulfillment of these prophetic words. He never ceased to help the suffering, defend the innocent, uphold the weak by the word of truth and faith, and to set himself as an example of all Christian virtues.

After the death of his parents, the whole of his rich heritage he gave in good works, endeavoring at that not to be known by those whom he befriended; for he remembered the commandment of God—to do good in secret, and not to seek for it the glory of men.

Here, for an instance, is one of the great many benefits shown by St. Nicholas.

A very rich citizen of Patara had suddenly lost the whole of his property, and fell into extreme poverty. Having been accustomed to riches, he did not find the strength to battle with the temptations of poverty, and he had commenced thinking already of procuring means for a living for himself and family, which consisted of three grown-up daughters, by a dishonorable practice. But he had not yet the opportunity of carrying out his evil intention, when he was saved by the timely help of St. Nicholas. Having heard of his troubles, St. Nicholas, under the cover of night, threw into his window a large amount of gold, tied up in a sack. On awakening in the morning, the unhappy father scarcely could believe that he unexpectedly became rich. His business was restored, and he soon gave his eldest daughter in marriage. St. Nicholas decided to settle in life the two other daughters in the same way, and after some time cast another sack of gold into the house of their father. The second daughter was honorably settled, and the happy father poured out before the

Lord his grateful feelings: "Merciful God, who redeemed us with Thy blood, and now saving me from sin and dishonor," thus he prayed, "show us the one who serves as the instrument of Thy goodness; show unto us this Thy earthly angel, who keeps us from sin, and delivers us from evil thoughts." This desire was granted. One night he heard the window opened, and the sound of a bundle thrown into the house, as before. He hurriedly arose, went in pursuit of his benefactor, and discovered Nicholas, who at that time administered the affairs of the diocese of Patara, in the absence of his uncle, who went to Jerusalem. He fell at his feet, and with tears of gratitude, he said: "If the Lord hath not sent you for our deliverance, I would not have withstood temptation, and would have enticed into sin and dishonor my innocent daughters."

After the return of his uncle, St. Nicholas himself went to pay his reverence at the tomb of our Lord, and during the voyage he stilled the stormy sea by his prayer, and brought to life a sailor who was killed by falling from the top of the mast. Continually growing more fervent in his love toward God, he settled in a monastery, desiring to devote his whole life to the Lord, and serve Him in the labors and privations of a monastic life. But the will of God prepared for him another field. One night, whilst praying, he all at once heard a voice say to him: "Nicholas, if thou wouldst have a crown from Me, enter thou in the way of labor among the populous crowd." In fear and doubt, Nicholas pondered about the meaning of such a calling. The same voice said again: "Nicholas, this is not the field in which you may reap the expected fruit. Turn to the people, that My name may be glorified in thee." Then it was that Nicholas understood that the Lord desired another service of him, in place of the monastic life he was leading. Submissive to the will of God, he left the place he had selected for his abode, and went to Myra, the principal city of Lycia, not knowing yet what the Lord would of him, but ready to fulfill His commandment.

At this time an election in Myra was taking place, in order to elect an archbishop in the stead of John, who died. Having gathered from all the cities, the bishops were anxious about the election. Understanding, of course, that God alone could enlighten and guide them, they therefore approached the election in prayer and fasting. The Lord heard their prayer, and to one of them he revealed His will. During prayer, a man, shining with a heavenly glory, appeared to this bishop, and told him to remain at the door of the church that night and to wait for the people. "The first one that enters," said he, "is the elected of God; his name is Nicholas." This bishop told this to the others, and stopped by the church doors, while the council of bishops were gathered in the church. In the mean time, St. Nicholas, having arrived in Myra, spent most of his time in prayer, and during this night, as usual with him, he went to the temple to hear matins. Hardly had he entered the door, when the bishop stopped him and inquired about his name. "Nicholas, the servant of your holiness, sir," he humbly answered. At that the bishop took him by the hand, and led him into the temple, where he placed him in the midst of the bishops. A rumor of this incident very soon spread around, and consequently a great multitude of people had come to the church. Having been strengthened by the vision, the bishop mentioned before addressed the people, and pointing out Nicholas, he said: "Brethren, accept your pastor, who is anointed by the Holy Ghost, and to whom He entrusted the ruling over your souls, who is elected, not by a body of men, but appointed by God." The people rejoiced, and thanked the Lord. St. Nicholas, in deep humility, did not consider himself worthy of so high a dignity, and he wished to refuse to accept the office, but he submitted to the will of God and became an archbishop.

Having become the pastor of the Church of Lycia, St. Nicholas, always strict unto himself, multiplied his labors with the thought that, in his new place, he must not live for himself, but for others. He selected two worthy presbyters to be his advisers and assistants, and with untiring devotion gave himself to care for those who were given to his charge. As a father, he received every one; he listened with sympathy to anybody's troubles, gave advice and help, and with strong determination defended the innocent and the ones offended. In the midst of such work he was taken by a sense of great danger which had come upon the Church, namely, the persecutions of the emperors Diocletian and Galerius. These fearful times of suffering lasted for ten years, and they were commenced in the city of Nicomedia, where about 20,000 Christians were burned to death while at prayer in the church. From this place the persecutions spread to every part of the empire. Not only in the cities and villages were Christians sought after, but they were hunted down in mountains and caves. Not fearing the danger, St. Nicholas continued to preach Christ, and therefore he was taken, with many Christians, and cast into prison, where they were kept for a long time, suffering hunger, thirst, and all sorts of trials. But the bishop, for all that, never ceased to console them with the Word of God. Now the Emperor Constantine came to the throne, and as he had known the true God, he gave all Christian prisoners their liberty. At the same time he destroyed the temples of the idols, and built many churches in honor of God Almighty. And so St. Nicholas was at liberty.

In the year A. D. 325, the first universal council of the Church was held. The chief object of this gathering was to testify to the truth against Arius, who impiously taught that the Son of God was made. Nicholas was one of the saints and teachers of the Church who had come to Nicea. Fervently testifying to the truth, he for a moment seemed to be transformed into a being resembling the Divine Wrath, when he struck a blow at the false mouth of the insolent Arius. For this act the holy fathers condemned him to be deprived of the episcopal insignia. But in the very same night many of the worthier ones had a vision, in which they saw the Lord Jesus Christ on the right side of St. Nicholas, who gave him the Book of the Gospels, and the most pure Mother of the Lord on the left of St. Nicholas, as she gave him the omophorion. By this it became known to them that the Lord Himself and His Holy Mother regarded Nicholas to be worthy of the holy office; they accordingly restored him, and thenceforth, nowithstanding his audacious conduct, they honored him as God's elect servant.

Soon after his return to his diocese, St. Nicholas saved from an unjust execution three citizens who were condemned to die by a wicked judge, who was bought over to the side of the false accusers by gold.

Among other good works and miracles performed by St. Nicholas, he at one time delivered from a criminal's death three army officers of high rank, who were under the ban of the emperor at Constantinople through suspicion aroused by envious persons. These three officers were personally acquainted with St. Nicholas. In their prayers to God, they mentioned Nicholas as a lover of justice, and, although St. Nicholas was a great distance away from them, he made his influence spiritually felt, through God's powerful grace, by the emperor and the prefect of Constantinople. He also saved some seafaring people in a storm; but when he noticed that they were addicted to bad habits, he admonished them in a way which made them repent. Wonderful was the power that his words had in winning the hearts of people; likewise his person, bright with the grace of God, influenced the very stubborn pagans, whom he converted. Many are the miracles of St. Nicholas, performed by him in sickness and other troubles of poor mankind, which are recorded in history, since the time in which he left this earthly abode, and of which we often hear in Russia, where many beautiful churches are dedicated to his blessed memory. He died in his very old age, and was buried in the cathedral of Myra, in the year 342. His holy body, which still seemed to be the temple of the Holy Ghost, was moist with a kind of aromatic oil, and Christians who were anointed with it in their sickness were healed.

THE LIFE OF ST. NINA, THE MISSIONARY OF GEORGIA.

January 14.

WE often see that God selects weak persons, such as are apparently incapable of accomplishing great and difficult works, for the purpose of fulfilling His will, and He makes them the agents who continue the work of the Saviour. And strengthened by the grace of God, they succeed in the labor and calling in which they are placed. No hardship should be considered too difficult in our good undertakings; only, in the commencement of a work, we should ask ourselves: Is the undertaking worthy of the Lord's blessing? and, if it be so, then we must undergo the labor with a firm hope in God's help, without which we may do nothing. It was a difficult task that the Lord committed to His disciples, when He commanded them to preach the Holy Gospel. Wise and learned men, nations, and kings arose up against the simple, untutored fishermen of Galilee, but the right hand of God upheld the Apostles, and the teaching of Christ spread rapidly, notwithstanding prohibitions and persecutions.

In the fourth century, to just such apostolical labor the Lord called a virgin; she was nothing more than a lonely, weak maiden, and her name was Nina. She was the niece of the patriarch of Jerusalem; in the holy city she obtained her education. From her young days she learned to love God with her whole heart. Understanding and feeling that the faith in an almighty and all-loving Heavenly Father was filled with grace; that it comforts man in sorrow; that it gives peace and a quiet firmness — Nina deeply felt for those who were still ignorant of the Holy Gospel. At this time, there were many countries with much people who were not as yet enlightened by the true religion; among them were the people who inhabited Eberia (*i. e.* the country now known as Georgia). Nina often heard the Jews speak about this land, when they came from thence to worship, in Jerusalem, on the feast of the Passover.

Repeated stories told about Eberia created in

Nina's heart a strong desire to visit Georgia (situated around the Caucasian Mountains), and enlighten the people with the Gospel teaching. She became encouraged in this desire by wonderful visions also. In a dream, she once saw the Mother of God, who gave her a cross made of grape-vines; at another time the Saviour appeared to her, and gave her a scroll, upon which she read the words, *Go and teach all nations, baptizing them in the name of the Father, and of the Son, and of the Holy Ghost* (Matt. xxviii: 19), the same as were addressed to the Apostles. Her desire was fulfilled. With a female acquaintance she went to Ephesus; here she found herself in the midst of the persecution which was carried on by the Emperor Diocletian. Compelled to flee, she found refuge in Armenia—in the abode of a certain Ripsimia. In the biography of St. Gregory, the great missionary of Armenia, we read, concerning this same Ripsimia, the following: " Ripsimia, who offered herself to the service of God, fled from the persecutions of Diocletian, and concealed herself in Armenia. Tiridat, the King of Armenia, endeavored to obtain her consent to a marriage with himself; but as he could not succeed in having her willingly leave her virginal life, he condemned her to a horrible death, together with her thirty-seven sister followers." By the mercy of God, Nina escaped the end of these Christian sisters. She fled to Eberia, the neighboring country. There is another tradition, which says that she was captured by some Eberian soldiers, who often made raids upon the surrounding country. However it may have been, still her arrival in Eberia served to evangelize that whole country. The Lord God did not cease to help her; He showed His wonders, creating miracles by her faithful word and hand, thereby bringing the whole race to the knowledge of Himself.

Soon after Nina's arrival in Eberia, there took place a great celebration in honor of one of the chief gods. Following the crowd, Nina came to the place where the idol stood, before which incense was burned, and sacrifices offered. Miriam, the king, together with his queen, the militia, and a multitude of people, was present at the feast, and reverently worshiped before the idol. Nina, with sorrow, looked upon the heathen holiday, and fervently prayed that

God might enlighten these people, who walked in the darkness of idol-worship. Suddenly, during a clear day, a mighty storm filled the air, and the idol fell, stricken by lightning. In fear, the crowd scattered, but Nina blessed the Lord, who answered her prayer by destroying the idol. This happened on the same day when Christians commemorate the Transfiguration of Jesus Christ.

After this, Nina went to live in the home of a woman who had her house in the king's vineyards, and it was not a very long while before she became known in the neighborhood, as she offered a miraculous assistance to all the suffering. The sick came to her in large numbers; she healed their diseases by her prayers, and taught them the true religion of the one God, who created the heavens and the earth, and she told them of Jesus Christ, who died for the salvation of the human race. The words of the stranger, the miracles which she performed, her life, all given up to prayer and good actions, greatly influenced the surrounding population, and many of them believed in God. Some of the people who were healed by Nina offered her rich gifts, and invited her to live with them; but the gifts she refused, and as to the poor hut in which she dwelled, she did not wish to depart from it, because the spot was sacred to her, through a tradition she had heard while yet in Jerusalem, from the Jews, who came there from this place. It was said that the cloak of the Lord Jesus was hidden in this same vineyard, and that it was brought hither in the following manner:

In the ancient past, as far back as the Babylonian captivity, several of the Jewish families, which were scattered into different countries, settled in Eberia. Sacredly preserving the ancient customs, they annually sent their selected men to Jerusalem to keep the Passover. The Jews of Eberia learned from these men that Jesus Christ was preaching in Jerusalem. They heard of His teaching, and of His miracles; they learned also that the scribes and the Pharisees hated Him, and that they sought to kill Him. These conversations aroused deep sympathy in the family of an old woman, who implored her son, with tears, not to take part in the unrighteous council against Jesus Christ, when he, Elioza, the old woman's son, was about to start on his journey to Jerusalem. While Elioza was in Jerusalem, Jesus Christ was delivered up. Elioza witnessed the sufferings of the Saviour, and he bought His (*i. e.* Jesus') cloak of the soldier who obtained it by the casting of lots. On his return home, the son did not find his mother among the living. Tradition tells, that at the same time when Christ the Saviour died on the cross, the old woman suddenly exclaimed: "The kingdom of Israel is no more!" and, with these words, she fell dead. Elioza was met by his young sister, Sidonia. When she saw the Lord's cloak in the hands of her brother, she quickly drew the sacred garment from him, and, pressing it to her breast, she died, then and there. They buried her in the king's garden, together with the cloak, which they could not loose from her embrace. On the spot of her grave, says tradition, a great cedar-tree grew up.

This cedar was in the vineyard where Nina now lived. Under its shade she often passed whole nights in prayer, beseeching God to bring the people of Eberia to the knowledge of Him. Wonderful visions strengthened her faith, revealing that she would be successful in this holy work. She saw, as it appeared to her, a flock of blackbirds flying from the king's garden, and, after washing in the waters of the Aragva, they became as white as snow, and from the high branches of the cedar they filled the surrounding country with heavenly music.

The wonders that were worked by Nina became heard of in all the land. It happened that the queen was taken sick; when she saw that the physicians could give her no assistance, she decided to send for the pious stranger, of whom she had heard so much. But Nina did not go to the royal palace; she invited the queen to come to her poor hut; and when she came, she recovered her health upon the prayer of Nina. "It is not I who heal thee, but Jesus Christ," said the religious recluse to the queen, "the Son of God, the Creator of the universe." The queen believed in the Lord. King Miriam, grateful for the healing of his consort, sent rich gifts to Nina; but she returned them, and sent word to the king that she had no desire for riches, only she hoped and wished that he would believe in the true God. A wonderful cure was also effected upon a relation of the king of Persia, who was a guest of Miriam's; and he also believed. Upon that, Miriam, fearing the anger of the king of Persia for the conversion of his relation, became dissatisfied with Nina, and decided to banish her; but the Lord showed His power upon the king himself, and turned his heart.

Once, while on a hunting tour, the king suddenly became enveloped by an impenetrable darkness; in fear, he called to his companions, but they, without interruption, continued the chase, not noticing anything, as the dark haze surrounded the king alone. At last, the king, in terror, thought of the words of Nina, and he called to God, whom Nina confessed. The darkness at once disappeared. Terrified by such a miracle, the king went to Nina; after obtaining instructions in the law of God, he believed with his whole heart, and decided to receive holy baptism. He sent to Constantinople with the intention of obtaining bishops and priests; he also commenced to build a church, upon the place where the sacred cedar stood, as Nina pointed out. The first timber put into the building was made out of the cedar-tree, and, likewise, four crosses were made out of it, which were sent to the different parts of the Iberian country. A number of wonders, which took place during the building of the new Christian temple, confirmed the faith in the Almighty God among the inhabitants.

The Emperor Constantine, who was converted to the true religion not long before this, by a miraculous appearance of the cross, made haste to send the patriarch of Antioch to Eberia. The patriarch consecrated a bishop for the new Christians. The first temple was dedicated in honor of the holy Apostles, and the Church of Eberia appointed the celebration, in honor of the discovery of the cloak of the Redeemer, to be on the first day of October.

Nina, who had no desire for honor and glory, went to live in a mountain; here, in seclusion, she offered her grateful praise to the Lord, who helped her to convert the idolaters. After some time, she left her seclusion, in order to continue her apostolical labors, and visited other parts of Eberia, where she converted to God, the queen of Kachetia, whose name was Sophia.

In this way, St. Nina worked as an apostle

for thirty-five years, when she felt that she would soon die; having sent for King Miriam and his wife, she blessed them, gave them her last instructions, and quietly gave up her soul to the Lord. In the place where she died, in Kachetia, Miriam built a church, which he dedicated in honor of the great martyr, St. George, who — according to tradition — was a relation to Nina, and he is considered to be the protector of Georgia.

A SAINTED BROTHER'S HISTORY OF A SAINTED SISTER.

THE histories of the lives of God's saints are precious to us. The stories relating to the way by which they reached the kingdom of heaven are instructive for us. But more instructing, more touching, are these stories when they are told, not by some unknown writer, but by God's holy ones,—the veritable witnesses of the truth. We offer our readers the sainted brother's story of a sainted sister,—the narrative about the holy Makrina, by St. Gregory, of Nice.

"Our parents named the child Makrina because there was a famous Makrina among our ancestors, namely, our father's mother, who suffered for Christ during the persecutions. The child was raised by its mother. Having passed the infant's age, she learned her childhood lessons with much zeal, and at the same time disclosed a rare talent. The mother took no pains in teaching her the worldly arts, but chiefly tried to have her acquire the wise sayings of Solomon and the Psalms. Did she arise from bed, or commence her work and finish the same; did she go to her meal, or leave the table; did she lie down to sleep, or kneel in prayer,—she continually had a song of the Psalms on her lips, and never was without it. And so Makrina reached her twelfth year, the age when the flower of youth especially begins to bloom. The fortunate beauty of the maiden could not be concealed, and many desiring to wed her came to her parents with their proposal. In the countries of the East, as is yet the custom, children are betrothed (not wedded) at an early age.

"The wise father selected one who came from a celebrated race, a young man known for his good morals, and to him he decided to wed his daughter when she became of age. But fate suddenly destroyed these beautiful hopes, snatching him away from this life at a much-to-be-mourned-for youthful age. Then it was the maiden decided to lead a lonely life; and when our parents would touch upon the question of matrimony, she would say that her betrothed did not die, but is alive with God; therefore, it is unreasonable for me to break the promise.

"She never separated from her mother, and the daughter's services substituted the work of many servants. The mother did service benefiting the maiden's soul, but she worked for her mother physically. For instance, she often prepared the bread for her mother, and took part in all the cares of the household, together with the mother, as the father had now left this life, and the mother had four sons and five daughters (Makrina being the eldest).

"When our mother settled her other daughters, there returned home to us, after a long absence at institutions of education, our brother, the great Basil (Basil the Great). Finding him thinking profoundly of oratory, Makrina soon attracted his attention to Christian philosophy, for which he cast aside the wordly vanity, and commenced a laborious ascetic life. Finally she induced our mother to lead the same kind of life, and she also commenced the pious labor on equal terms with the virgins. Their life was so holy that I do not know how to describe it.

"Reaching a very old age, our mother died on the hands of her children. In the ninth year of his prelacy the eminent Basil goes to God. Hearing of this from a distance, Makrina's soul sorrowed much for this great loss. Yet, under such weighty strokes of misfortune, she remained as firm as an invincible warrior. Soon after this, I, Gregory, became desirous of visiting my sister; for, during eight years, severe circumstances which I suffered prevented the meeting before.

"On the day before my arrival at the place where she lived, I had a vision in a dream; it seemed as though I carried on my hands the relics of a martyr, and from the relics shone forth such a light that I could not look upon them. I saw the same three times in one night. A kind of melancholy filled my soul.

"Coming near to the abode of my sister, I questioned one whom I met about my sister. He told me that she was sick. I hurried; my heart seemed to shrink away. When I entered her sacred apartment [*cell*, in the original], I found her not lying on a bed, or on a litter, but on the floor, on a board covered with a hair cloth; another board, placed slantingly, served as a pillow. Raising herself on her elbow,—for now she could not get up—she offered me the salutation at meeting. I ran to her, consoled her, and helped her back again; then, outstretching her arms towards heaven, she said: 'And this joy also Thou didst grant me, O God! Thou didst not deprive me of what I so desired; Thou didst send Thy servant [minister] to visit Thy handmaid.' To lighten our sorrow on her account, she tried to conceal the difficulty of her breathing; forcing herself to smile, she talked of pleasant things, telling us of all that happened to her since her childhood, as if she read from a book. She blessed God from the bottom of her soul for all His mercies. I commenced to tell of how much I suffered when I was exiled for the faith by the Emperor Valent; but she said: 'Will you not cease being ungrateful towards God? He rewarded you with His favors more than our parents. They say that you are become known to cities and whole provinces; they summons you and send you to aid the Church. . . . You must know that the prayers of parents elevate one to such a height.' Listening to her, I was sorry to see the day declining towards evening. After the nocturnal prayers and rest, when the morning came, it became clear to me that this morning was the last for the sick one; the fever consumed the remaining strength of the sufferer. My soul was full of sadness, because the tenderness of my sister called forth softness on my part for her—a saint; but, at the same time, I wondered at the ineffable tranquillity with which she awaited the end. The sun was nearly setting, but the happy state of her spirit did not leave her. She stopped speaking to us, and her eyes fixed towards heaven (her poor couch was turned towards the east), she sweetly and softly conversed with the Lord, so that with difficulty we could catch some of the words. 'Thou, O Lord,' she said, ' destroyed for us the fear of death. . . . Thou givest rest to our bodies in sleep of death, and again awakenest them at the sound of the trumpet at the end of ages. . . . O Eternal God, to whom I belong from the womb of my mother, whom I love with all my soul, to whom I gave my body and soul!

Grant me a bright angel who would bring me to the holy fathers in the place of freshness and repose. . . . Thou that forgavest one of them that were crucified with Thee, having only recourse to Thy mercy, remember me also in Thy kingdom. . . . . May not the spirit-envier prevent me from fleeing to Thee; let all my sins disappear before Thee. Thou that hast the power to forgive sins, forgive the sins of my weakness, and receive my soul as a blessing before Thee!'

"Saying these words, she made the sign of the cross over her mouth, eyes, and heart. . . . It became dark; the candles were brought in; she opened her eyes and began to repeat the Psalms, but her voice failed her, and she continued her prayer mentally. Having finished, she tried to raise her arm, in order to make the sign of the cross,—a deep, heavy sigh came from her breast, and her life ended, together with her prayer!

"Until now all who surrounded her remained silent, suppressing their emotion; but now there were to be heard wailings, and I myself wept bitterly. . . . But glancing on her that fell asleep, and, as if chided by her for the disorder, I sent them all out, leaving such of my sister's fellow workers as were the most intimate. One of them, by name Vestiana, clothing the poor body of Makrina with vestments, called me, and disclosing a part of the breast, while showing with the light of a candle, she said to me: 'Do you see that hardly visible mark? Once there appeared on that spot a painful swelling, and danger threatened lest the disease should reach the heart. Her mother often begged her to consult medical advice. But she, deeming the baring of any part of the body before a stranger's eyes more unwholesome than the disease, did not agree to do so.

"'Withdrawing to the church [temple] she remained there all night in prayer, and mingling her prayerful tears with the earth, she put this tearful dust to the sore breast instead of medicaments. And to her mother she said that it would be enough for her if she, her mother, would make with her own hand a sign of the cross over the swelling. Her mother satisfied her desire; the sore disappeared, and here— in remembrance of this grace of God—there remained only this mark.'

"Vesting the reposed one [Oriental expression—is it not appropriate?], Vestiana found on her neck a small iron cross and ring attached to a cord. 'Let us divide the inheritance,' said I; 'keep for yourself the saving cross, and for me this ring is sufficient, as on its stamp there is the sign of the cross also.' 'You did not make a mistake,' said Vestiana, 'for in this ring there is a particle of the life-giving wood.'

"Tidings of the demise of the revered one brought a multitude of people of all classes to the abode [convent]. So did the bishop of that place come with the clergy. Slowly and with appropriate hymns did we, the ministers of the altar, bear the funeral bier to the Church of the Holy Martyrs; where the body of my sister was laid by the side of our mother's remains, according to the desire of them both. . . . Once more I prostrated myself before the coffin, and, kissing the remains, in sorrow and tears I left the church."

ST. JOHN CHRYSOSTOM.

THIS great teacher, on account of the fluency and sweetness of his eloquence, obtained the surname of Chrysostom, or Golden-Mouth, which we find given him by St. Ephrem, Cassiodorus, and others. But his tender piety, and his undaunted courage and zeal in the cause of virtue, are titles far more glorious, by which he holds an eminent place among the greatest pastors of the Church. He was born during the first half of the fourth century in the city of Antioch. His mother, Anthusa, left a widow at twenty years of age, continued such the remainder of her life, dividing her time between the care of her family and the exercises of devotion. From their cradle, she instilled into her children the most perfect maxims of piety, *and contempt of the world.* The better class of Romans, as well as the ancient Greeks, dreaded nothing more in the education of youth, than their being ill taught the first principles of the sciences. Therefore Anthusa provided her son the ablest masters in every branch of literature which the empire at that time afforded. The progress of the young scholar surprised the philosophers. Yet, all this time, his principal care was to study Christ, and to learn His Spirit. He laid a solid foundation of virtue, by a perfect humility, self-denial, and a complete victory over himself.

Our saint, by circumstances ordered by the Lord, left the desert, where he abode for a number of years, and returned to the city. Bishop Flavian, foreseeing the Church's good fortune and opportunity, ordained John to the priesthood, at the same time making him his vicar and preacher. The saintly ascetic had reached by this time his forty-third year. Now, as a champion of the truth, his fame spread throughout the empire. It seemed as if nothing could withstand the united power of his eloquence, zeal, and piety.

St. Chrysostom had been five years deacon, and twelve years priest, when Nectarius, Bishop of Constantinople, dying in 397, the Emperor Arcadius, at the suggestion of Eutropius the eunuch, his chamberlain, resolved to procure the election of John to the patriarchate of the royal city. He therefore dispatched a secret order to the Viceroy of the East, enjoining him to send John to Constantinople, but by some stratagem, lest his intended removal, if known at Antioch, should be opposed to by his devoted flock. On being brought to Constantinople, although it was against his will, John was consecrated archbishop for the capital— with the powers of a patriarch in that whole region. It might be expected that John, a holy man of God, had enemies who were on the alert to injure him, either personally, or by defaming his noble character. Among such was Theophilus, Patriarch of Alexandria, who strove against the elevation of John.

On becoming the chief-pastor in this new charge, our saint turned his attention first toward the helpless and poor sufferers, for whom he founded hospitals and asylums. It was the body of clergy next which caused him much anxiety and watch in his endeavors to keep it at the height of its calling. Nothing escaped the eagle eye of this zealous teacher of Christianity. Knowing well the importance of the position held in society by the mothers, wives, and sisters of homes, he addressed the ladies and women of Constantinople who neglected to cover their necks, or used a foolish and unnatural fashion of dress, in this way: "Immoral persons hide their baits at home only for the wicked; but you," said he, "carry your snares everywhere, and spread your nets publicly in all places. You allege that you never invited others to sin. You did not by your tongue, but you have done it by your dress and manners more effectually than you could by your voice. When you have made another sin in his heart, how can you be innocent? You sport yourselves in the ruin of the souls of others, and make their spiritual death your pastime."

As at Antioch St. John did, he likewise suppressed the wicked custom of swearing in Constantinople. His eloquence and zeal combined tamed the fiercest sinners, and changed them into meek lambs; he also converted a large number of idolaters and heretics. To the repentant he was a most tender father. On one occasion, his indignation was roused, we can fearlessly say, to a height which was divinely inspired, by some professed Christians who desecrated the holy days by leaving the house of prayer to go to see horse-races, and then, only a short time after they had implored in humility for God's mercy to stop the heavy rainfall, which endangered the grain crop. The holy bishop appealed to the sinners: "Are these things to be borne? Can they be tolerated?" The saint grieved the more, because, after all, they said they had done no harm, though they had murdered not only their own souls, but also those of their children. "And how will you," said he, " after this, approach the holy place? How will you touch the heavenly food? Even now do I see you overwhelmed with grief, and covered with confusion."

St. John laid out to the poor all his revenues. His own patrimony he had given to the poor, long before, at Antioch. This great man's labors and influence became felt in the remotest countries of the earth. He sent a bishop to instruct the nomads, or wandering Scythians; another to the Goths, and so on. He was himself endued with an eminent spirit of prayer; this he knew to be the great channel of heavenly blessings, the cleanser of the affections of the soul from earthly dross, and the means which renders men spiritual and heavenly, and makes them angels, even in their mortal body.

In the mean time, the enemies of the holy Chrysostom were lying in wait for their victim. They succeeded in gaining the favor of the imperial court—especially those members of it who accused John for personal insult, because for such did their lame conscience take his expositions of the commandments of God. The good patriarch was banished. Twice was he compelled to leave Constantinople. Now, in his old age, when sickness and physical pains seized him, he was forced to travel on foot in the night-time. Being deprived of every necessary of life, he was greatly refreshed if he got a little clear water to drink, fresh bread to eat, or a bed to take a little rest upon. But all he lamented was the impenitence of his enemies—for their own sake. Finally, the soldiers reached as far as to Cucusus, and here they left him to the mercy of the simple villagers. This poor town in Armenia was not the home of the sufferer for any length of time. His letters from this place could reach the great cities; and, truly, they did thrill the souls of many thousands of the faithful. This great light of the Church, who enlightened the path of so many Christians, could not be endured by a few impious enemies. They resolved to rid the world of him. Two officers were dispatched to convey him to the distant shores of the Black Sea. They led the old bishop over very rough roads, under a scorching sun. When they arrived at Comana Pontica, he was very sick. Seeing him in a dying condition, they left him with the priest of that place. Now, in this place the relics of the martyr St. Basilicus rested. This saint appeared to John at night, and said to him: "Be of good cheer, brother John; to-morrow we shall be together." The good pastor was filled with joy at this news, and begged that he might stay there till the following day. He washed and prepared himself as if for a great feast. He received the holy sacrament of the Lord's Supper, and shortly after gave up his pure soul with these words: *Glory be to God for all things.*

SOMETHING ABOUT AN EVENING HYMN.

> O Joyful Light, of the holy
> Glory of the Immortal Father;
> Heavenly, Holy, Blessed Jesus Christ,
> We — having come to the setting of the sun—
> Beholding the evening light,
> Hymn our God, the Father, Son, and Holy Ghost—
> Worthy art Thou at all times
> To be hymned with reverent voices,
> O Son of God, Giver of life:
> Wherefore the world glorifieth Thee.
>   [VESPER HYMN—ORTHODOX CHURCH.]

BEAUTIFUL words! What a fullness of expression this soft Light, that came even unto the setting of the sun, conveys to us, inhabitants of the extreme West, Christians—who live just where the sun goes down after shining over the last continent of earth. I wish all of you could enjoy the sweetness of harmonious phraseology that glides all through this sublime hymn, as we have it in the Greek, or in its Slavonic translation. The poetry suffers in order to preserve the sense of the original words when translated into the English. But the thought itself is so elaborate that you catch a faint echo of the sacred music.

The reason why this hymn is appropriated to evening devotion is plainly expressed in the hymn itself. The thought of Christ, the soft Light, is naturally called forth at sight of the sunset and the mellow light of lamps. *Christ, by the Godhead, is an ever-existing Light, as He is the eternal brightness of God the Father, and the express image of His Being* (Heb. i: 3). But for the salvation of humankind, He concealed His Divine glory beneath the form of a man, and in this way He became as the soft light of the evening. A comparison very striking! The haze that generally fills the evening air lessens the brightness of the sunlight. In the daytime the light of the sun is unbearable, so that one cannot look at it with an unarmed eye. But look at the same sun in the evening, and see how softly he shines. Every one may look at him plainly, admire his beauty, and the beauty of those gorgeous pictures that he forms in the clouds by the reflection of his light. And thus it is that the Son of God, unapproachable according to His divinity, has made Himself accessible to us by His humanity, through which the light of His Godhead had lessened so that we could see the Word of life with plain eyes, hear and feel Him (John i: 1); and having made Himself accessible for all, He also made the way approachable for all, through Himself, to the Heavenly Father, the Holy, the Blessed, so that they who have seen the Son have seen the Father Himself (John xv: 9).

The Eastern light has come to the West— to the uttermost Western end! And blessed be they who, with a clear vision, perceive this light just as it shines in the East. This light, although it came from the East, did not change, but while it shines in the West, it continues to be the light of the East; it is the Eternal Light. Christ, who is the East Himself, laid down Himself as the chief cornerstone of His Church, which he established in the East, and they in the West who receive this light of the East, must so shine as the light of the East would have them be enlightened; but not allow themselves to be dazzled with the glare of a false fire; I say *fire*, but not *light*, as no light cometh from the West. Praise and glorify the Good God! See, He comes to the West from the East, that all may see by that One Light, and be saved in the bond of union, which is Love!

For many centuries this evening hymn has been heard in Christian temples; nor has it through all these ages, nor in the temples, lost its freshness and tenderness. It seems, rather, that with every going-down of the sun it becomes new again; at every eventide to which it pleases God to prolong our life it may stimulate our souls with new vigor, with holy thoughts, with heavenly aspiring emotion. Do we sing this praise ourselves, or do we hear others hymn, we always feel a hallowed sweetness of heart, an elevated feeling inspires the soul. But where does the evening sun go? He does not fade away; but, hidden from us, he lights up with the same brightness the other side of our earth. And so, without a doubt, does our spiritual sun, which is hidden from our eyes, always, and in like manner, shine and is seen in all His glory in another world, whereas here the eye of faith may see only the reflection of His never-setting Light.

The historic tradition which tells how this hymn was composed is most interesting: On one of the hills of Jerusalem—very likely on the same mount from which the Saviour of the world looked down upon Jerusalem in the mellow twilight, and sorrowfully conversed with His disciples of the approaching fall of the city of God—there sat, all alone, an old man, wise old Sophronius; he was the Bishop of Jerusalem —patriarch of the earliest Eastern Church: he sat, and his meditative gaze was fixed on the setting sun of Palestine. The profound stillness, the fading light of the evening, the cool and invigorating air, and other impressive pictures of nature at eventide, with which the wise Sophronius loved to enjoy himself, so fixed the attention of the servant of God that he fell into a deep meditation. Before him lay Jerusalem, with which great memories of so much is connected; the rays of the sun now, as oft before, fell on that glorious city, but they never more shone down in it to light up the temple of Solomon, nor the palace of Herod, nor the strong walls and high towers of Sion. It looked dreary and desolate,—as desolate as it is in a house when the host, dead a long time, leaves no one to keep house after him. The wise Sophronius did not grieve for the ruins of the walls and temple of Jerusalem. He knew that from the fragments of the old the new Jerusalem arose, which shone out in all the world, and over which shineth the glory of the Lord; for he had once, before becoming patriarch, with a pilgrim's staff, wended his way through Greece, Palestine, Syria, Egypt; seeing everywhere Christian cities, and everywhere finding temples consecrated to the name of the Saviour.

And so the evening light, softly falling over the remains of the ancient Jerusalem, directs the thought of the wise, grand old man and prelate to objects of more importance than the ruins of the city. As Elias of old *in the still small voice* (1 Kings xix: 12) recognized the presence of Jehovah, so does old Sophronius, philosopher and historian, orator and poet, patriarch and saint all at the same time, in the soft light of the evening twilight, mentally feel the touch of another, higher Light. The material sun, declining in the West, inclines the mind of the bishop to conceive the immaterial sun,—and the image of the holy, life-conceiving Trinity, was borne before his spiritual eyes. The Western destination of the sun brought to his memory the gloomy West of the fallen nature of mankind; the soft light of the setting sun, softly bathing in its rays tired nature at eventide, lively represents to him the descent of the Son of God unto dark humanity, that He may enlighten and resurrect it, and with it all nature. In the cool breath of the evening air he perceives the type of that grace by which the Holy Ghost, in consequence of the redemption accomplished on the Cross by Jesus Christ, quickens and spiritualizes man and the universe. The soul of the wise old man abounds in pious emotion, and with a trembling voice, a saintly voice, he sings an evening hymn to the Creator of the universe: O Thou soft Light of the holy glory! O Christ, my Saviour! Thou that revealed unto us the glory of the Heavenly Father! O soft Light of the holy glory, upon which the spiritual eye so loves to gaze, as the eyes of the body upon the mellow twilight! Thou wouldst save the world, and Thou hast come once upon a time unto the dark West—yea, even down unto our nature; therefore, each time when we reach the going-down of the sun, day by day, when we behold the light of the evening, we praise Thy Father, Thee the Son we praise, praise we the Holy Ghost, glorifying the Triune God. O Son of God, that givest life unto us and all creatures! we should sing to Thee with reverential voices, we should fall down before Thee not only at the setting of the sun, nor only when we see the twilight, but at all times of the day and the year. Thou art the life of the world, and Thee therefore the whole world glorifies. Amen.

THE LIFE OF ST. PELAGIA.

SAINT PELAGIA was born at the close of the fourth century, or at the very beginning of the fifth century. She lived at Antioch, which at that time was one of the richest and greatest cities of the whole East. The extraordinary beauty of Pelagia drew many admirers after her. She did not marry, but occupied herself by entertaining the pleasure-seeking crowds in public places. Her house was open to rich lovers. It happened at this time that several bishops had come to Antioch to hold a conference, together with the archbishop of the capital. Among them was Nonnus, the Bishop of Heliopolis. The prelates were lodged in the neighborhood of the Church of St. Julian the Martyr. One day, whilst they were sitting before the church with Nonnus, whom they were questioning, and whom they listened to with much attention, for he was a wise and holy man, Pelagia came down along the street and passed before them in great pomp, decked with gold, pearls, and precious stones, accompanied by a numerous train of young men, women, and servants. Her beauty, with the lustre of her jewels and rich attire, drew the eyes of all the fond admirers of these empty toys upon her; but whilst the prelates turned aside their faces, because having no veil over her head, and her very shoulders being uncovered, they were offended at the immodesty of her dress, Nonnus only seemed to take notice of her, and to consider her with great attention. After she had passed by, turning to his fellow bishops, he said to them, with many sighs and tears: "I fear God will one day bring this woman to confront us before the throne of His justice, in order to condemn our negligence and tepidity in His service, and in the discharge of our duty to the flock He has committed to our care. For how many hours do you think she has employed this very day in washing and dressing herself, adorning and embellishing her whole person to the best advantage, with a view to exhibit her beauty to please the eyes of the world, which to-day is, but to-morrow passes away? Whereas we, who have an Almighty Father, an immortal Spouse in heaven, His Son, and the sanctifying Holy Ghost, in whose name we were baptized, and whom we should serve — we, to whom the immense and eternal treasures of Heaven are promised as the reward of our short labors upon earth, are far from taking as much pains to wash and purify our souls from their stains, and procure for them those bright ornaments of virtue and sanctity which alone can render them truly agreeable in the eyes of God." Having spoken to this effect, St. Nonnus returned home, and, prostrating himself, implored the divine mercy for the forgiveness of his negligence.

On the next day the bishops assembled in the great church to offer the liturgy. St. Nonnus was requested by the archbishop to deliver an exhortation to the people. Strange as it may seem, it happened that on this very day Pelagia visited the cathedral. The bishop's sermon was on repentance. His words, inspired by a holy unction, made so deep an impression on her soul that she could not refrain the whole time from sighing and shedding tears, through the deep sense she conceived of her sins. As soon as the divine service was over, she sent a letter to the holy prelate, begging him to receive her into the fold of those who seek salvation. Nonnus sent her word that if she was sincere in her desires of instruction and conversion, she might come to him to the Church of St. Julian, where he would receive her, but on condition to speak with her in the presence of the other bishops. When Pelagia received this permission, she came with all speed, and cast herself at the feet of the holy man, earnestly beseeching him, through the example of his great Master, Jesus Christ, to receive the worst of sinners, and cleanse her from the filth and abomination of her crimes in the fountain of baptism. Nonnus told her that she must first be tried, to assure the Church of her sincerity. But she would not arise from the floor, where she continued to weep bitterly, and repeatedly promising to be a new creature if they would but take her away from the power of the Devil. Thus she was allowed to be baptized, all the bishops witnessing her repentance and approving. The Patriarch of

Antioch sent Romana, the first deaconess of his diocese, to be godmother to Pelagia. The hope in the mercy of God which this great sinner had was marvelous. And for the love of Jesus Christ she was saved.

After her baptism, Pelagia, having taken an inventory of all her plate, jewels, rich clothes, and other goods, put it into the hands of St. Nonnus, saying: "Reverend Father! here are the goods I acquired from the Devil; take them, and do what you will with them. As for me, I now desire nothing but the grace of my Saviour, Jesus Christ." The saint delivered the inventory into the hands of the treasurer of the Church, and charged him, as he would answer for it before God, not to apply any part of her property either to the service of the clergy or the Church, but to distribute the whole to poor widows and orphans, and such like charities; that as they had been ill-gotten, they might now at least be well applied. At the same time, Pelagia set all her slaves at liberty, earnestly exhorting them to shake off that yoke of servitude by which they, as well as herself, had been slaves to a corrupt world.

On the eighth day, when those who had been

baptized, according to the ancient custom of the Church, put off the white garment they received at their baptism, Pelagia rising privately in the night, exchanged her baptismal robe for a habit of haircloth, and without communicating her design to any one but Him, she withdrew from Antioch, and going into the Holy Land, took up her habitation in a narrow cell upon Mount Olivet, where she lived as a hermit, shut up in such a manner as to have only a small window through which she might receive necessary food, and spending her whole time with the Lord in fasting and prayer. The other religious inhabitants of this holy mountain were so perfectly ignorant who she was, as not even to know whether she was a woman, so effectually had she concealed her sex, calling herself by the name of *Pelagius;* but they all admired the great austerity and sanctity of her life.

Not many years after this, James, a deacon of the Church of Heliopolis, paid a visit of devotion to the sepulcher of our Lord at Jerusalem. This James had seen Pelagia before; for he was with St. Nonnus at the time of her conversion. While in the Holy Land he profited himself by visiting celebrated monasteries, and obtaining advice and information from the holy fathers who led a secluded life. In this way he found Pelagia, to whom he had come for a blessing, not knowing who she was. St. Pelagia spoke to him for a few moments through her small window, but soon closed it, for her time to pray came with the third hour. Before returning home from Palestine, James resolved to see once more the holy hermit. On coming to her cell, he knocked at the window. No one opened it to him; and when he called no one answered. After calling and knocking for a long time, he forced open the window, and looking in he perceived the saint to be dead. Having conveyed the news of her death to the neighboring religious, they immediately came, and opening the cell took out the body, in order to its being interred with all the honor due to so great a servant of God. The secret of her sex being now discovered and noised abroad, all the holy virgins that dwelt on the banks of the Jordan, came out with lighted candles in their hands, singing the Psalms at her funeral. The Church celebrates the memory of St. Pelagia on the 8th of October.

SAINTS CYRIL AND METHODIUS, THE APOSTLES OF THE SLAVONIANS.

May 11.

IT is with gratitude and reverence that we mention the names of St. Cyril and his brother Methodius, the first teachers of the Slavonic people, who gave us the Word of God in the Slavonian language. "God, in His mercy, gives to every race and time its teachers, and to us He gave Constantine (and his brother Methodius), who enlightened our people." This is the way in which an old Slavonic history commences to relate the life of the philosopher Constantine (the name Cyril was given him not long before his death, in taking the final vows of an ascetic), who was the inventor of the Slavonian alphabet, and the preacher of the Word of God in the Slavonic countries. Constantine (or Cyril) lived in the ninth century; he was the youngest son of a rich and noted nobleman of the Greek city of Salonica. His father's name was Leo, and his mother's Mary. The family was a large one; and it was brought up in all gravity, according to the faith. The Greek emperor installed Methodius, the elder brother, as governor of the Slavonic tribes, which, at that time, lived in the neighborhood of Salonica. But, after a few years, Methodius desired to leave the world. He left the Slavonic principality, after which he settled in Mount Olympus, where he was tonsured a monk, and devoted his days in prayer and the study of the Holy Scriptures.

In the mean time, Constantine was occupied with his studies in the homes of his parents. While yet a little boy, he saw in his dreams that the ruler of the city had once gathered a great many maidens, and told him to select for himself a bride; at that, he selected the most beautiful one; her name was *Sofia*. Now the meaning of this name is *wisdom*. Constantine truly did obtain wisdom, for he was clever and diligent in his studies. One of the eminent tutors of the young Emperor Michael, in Constantinople, had heard of the bright lad,

Constantine, for he knew the family of Salonica. On securing the parents' consent, he at once sent for the boy, to study with the young emperor in the palace. Under the guidance of the most learned men of the empire, but especially the celebrated Photius (who after became the Patriarch of Constantinople), the young man made rapid progress in his studies, which gained for him the name of *Philosopher*. But Constantine was not taken with pride, nor did he make a display of his learning and title.

When he had reached the full age of manhood, Constantine was appointed librarian of the cathedral of Santa Sophia. He did not remain long in this position, however; for, renouncing all ties, he secretly left the city, and became a monk in a monastery not far from the Bosphorus. But he was soon found out, and after the emperor's personal request, he consented to return to the metropolis. At the age of twenty-four, he was sent as an envoy from the court of Constantinople to the ruler of the Saracens. Constantine's position was a very dangerous one, as the Mahometans, proud in their victories and growing possessions, and as ignorant fanatics, especially at this time, were most dangerous to the personal safety of Christians. The religious leaders of the Saracens confronted our Christian philosopher with the question: "Why is it, that among you Christians, who worship one God, there are so many differences in faith and in life, while we Mahometans strictly adhere to one law, and do not transgress it?" "Our God," replied Constantine, "is as a vast ocean, whose depth is immeasurable, inconceivable to the human mind. Many probe into the immense greatness, seeking for the Lord; some, strong in mind and faith, and supported by the grace of God, find riches of wisdom and salvation; others, weak, and deprived of the help of God for their pride and self-conceitedness, endeavor to sail across this vast region, but they fail for the want of strength; they either get lost or exhausted by the hardships. God, having created man, adorned him with a free will. He may select his way; he may rise with his mind, and resemble the angels, serving God and fulfilling His law. He also may lower himself to the equal of animal, feeding his desires, and binding himself in passions. In order to serve God, one must struggle with himself; he must endeavor to grow in perfection, to conquer his passions, and bridle his evil habits; but this is a difficult task. Now, your religion, as a small stream, is comprehensible to any one; everything in it is human, and nothing divine. It does not demand of you any struggles or hardships. It does not make it your duty to constantly advance to a higher perfection, and, therefore, it is easily accessible to any one; without any labor one may fulfill the whole of your law."

After his return home, Constantine went to live with his brother Methodius, in Mount Olympus. Away from the vanities of the world, they constantly strengthened themselves in wisdom and in the faith, going deeper into the study of Christ's law. Not a very long time went by thus, when the holy brothers were called forth to live and work among the people. They were sent as missionaries by the Church at Constantinople to convert the people living along the northern coast of the Black Sea, and who were called Chozars. It took considerable time for them to master the language. The missionaries worked incessantly. Their labors were made the heavier for the opposition that the Jews and Samaritans showed them, who also greatly strove to convert the inhabitants. St. Cyril was constantly occupied in sharp disputes; but St. Methodius aided none the less, by his fervent prayers to God. And God blessed the work of the brothers. The prince of the Chozars believed, and was baptized. A large number of people immediately followed his example. When Sts. Methodius and Cyril were about to return to Constantinople, the prince would have them accept rich gifts; but they refused to accept anything in return for the grace of God in the Gospel, which they had brought to the people, and in place of the gifts, they requested that some Greek captives be given their freedom. On their way, the brothers visited another tribe living by the Sea of Azov. This people they also brought to Christ. The missionaries were triumphantly greeted in Constantinople as apostles. These true servants of the Saviour would accept no honors or dignity. St. Cyril took up his living by the Church of the Holy Apostles, and

St. Methodius became the abbot of a monastery.

It was about this time that the sister of Boris, the king of Bulgaria, had returned home from Constantinople, where she was held a captive. Being now a Christian, she prevailed upon the king to at least apply to Byzantium for learned teachers in the faith. St. Methodius at once went over to Bulgaria, and in a comparatively short time had converted Boris, who, through his sister, was already acquainted with the teaching of the Gospel.

Soon after this, Rostislav and Sviatopolk, princes of Moravia, and Kotsel, a prince of Blaten (*i. e.* in Pannonia, which is the country we know now as Hungary), petitioned the emperor of Constantinople to send them a bishop and teacher. The emperor referred the matter to the patriarch, who at that time was the celebrated Photius. At a council of bishops it was decided to give this great undertaking to the charge of Sts. Cyril and Methodius, as to such who were from Salonica, and consequently who knew the Slavonic language. Notwithstanding his failing health, St. Cyril agreed to go to those who were seeking the truth. He was anxious that the Christian religion should take a firm hold upon the many kindred tribes of a young but great race of people. For this purpose he put to the emperor the question: "Have not the Slavonians any letters?" "Both my grandfather and father sought for them, but did not find any," answered the emperor. "How can I preach to them?" said St. Cyril; "it is the same as though one wrote upon the waters. If I should invent letters myself, I fear I may be called a false teacher." "The Lord will guide thee and give thee His help," replied the emperor.

Firm in the hope of obtaining God's blessing for his labors, St. Cyril set himself to the task of constructing an alphabet for the Slavonic people, that they may retain the Word of God written down for them, as teaching by word merely could soon become forgotten. He very earnestly prayed, besides putting himself under an obligation of fasting for forty days; and shutting himself in his cell with a few disciples, who were to share in his future apostolic journey, he commenced the work of inventing letters. In this way the Slavonic alphabet had its origin. The language now being adapted to writing, St. Cyril translated the Gospel of St. John for the first book. The first words written in the Slavonian language were these: *In the beginning was the Word, and the Word was with God, and the Word was God.*

When this great work had been accomplished, A. D. 862, the whole religious council, at a grand public praise, gave thanks to the Lord. The philosopher Constantine was now consecrated a bishop, and, in company with his brother Methodius and several disciples, he went to the Slavonic countries. He carried a letter to Prince Rostislav from the Emperor Michael, which read as follows: "The Lord, who commands every one to learn the truth, hath wrought a great work by showing your language in letters. We send to you the same honorable man through whom the Lord gave this writing, a philosopher both religious and very learned. He carries to you a gift more valuable than gold and precious stones. Help him to confirm and promote your language, and seek God, not minding the labor of any undertaking; and thyself, having brought thy people to the mind of God, wilt receive thy reward in this age, and in that which is to come."

The brothers' teaching went on prosperously. During four years and a half they went through all Moravia and Pannonia, calling on the people to believe in the one true God, and explaining for them His law. Prince Kotsel himself began to learn to read and to study the Slavonic language, while he recommended fifty young men to study with St. Cyril. This new apostle, untiring in labor for the benefit of his neighbors, translated the Book of Psalms, a part of the Bible, and all the Church services into the Slavonic language. Now divine worship was offered in the Slavonian countries in a language which was understood by all, while in the Roman Catholic countries the Latin language is used in the Church services up to this day. As it was before, in converting the Chozars, likewise on this occasion St. Cyril would take no gifts or acknowledgments from the new Christians for his labors; but he begged Prince Kotsel to liberate nine hundred captives.

Such was the beginning of the spread of Christian learning by the newly invented literature of the Slavonic language. The grammar of this language was formed principally for the purpose of explaining and spreading the Word of God; from its birth it was the instrument of true civilization. When St. Cyril intrusted this most precious gift (*i. e.* the Word of God) to the Slavonian people in their own language, he said to them in his preface to the Gospel: " Ye Slavonian peoples, hear ye the Word which feeds the soul of man, the Word which strengthens the heart and mind." God grant that our literature always remains worthy of its holy origin; that it may serve a good purpose in explaining the law of God, science, and true wisdom!

Sts. Cyril and Methodius, as other Christian evangelists, suffered not a little from calamities and persecutions. German and Latin bishops, who also preached to this people, envied the work of the orthodox brothers, and they arose against the translation of the Holy Scriptures into the Slavonic tongue. They said that the Gospel should be read only in the three tongues, which writings were nailed to the cross of Jesus Christ, viz: Hebrew, Greek, and Latin. St. Cyril replied that, as the Lord came upon the earth for the salvation of all people, consequently all should glorify and thank Him, and strive to understand His will. He said that God, in His mercy, gives the air and rain for all, and commands the sun to shine for all; thus, therefore, He does not desire to deprive any one of a greater gift, *i. e.* to know and understand His will.

But the bishops would not accept this answer, and they complained to the Pope against the teachers of the Slavonians. It was about this time that the great division in the Church began to show itself. The Greek Church, which remained faithful to orthodoxy, did not approve of the innovations introduced into the Latin Church, and opposed chiefly an unnecessary and heretical addition to the Creed itself, and the tendency of the Roman clergy to attain temporal power. Besides this, there was a misunderstanding between the Patriarch of Constantinople and the Pope of Rome concerning the young Church of Bulgaria; but as yet there was no open rupture, and the Church now as before continued to recognize, not the power of the Roman bishop, but his precedence, as the first among equals. Therefore, Sts. Cyril and Methodius, obeying the summons, went to Rome for an explanation. They took with them a part of the relics of St. Clement, who was one of the first bishops of the early Church in Rome. These relics the holy brothers brought from the shores of the Black Sea, where St. Clement was drowned by order of the Emperor Trajan. On their way the missionaries taught the Slavonian people in their own language, and in Venice they were challenged to dispute with the Latins.

In the mean time Pope Nicholas had died. His successor, Adrian II., who endeavored to restore harmony and peace to the Church, did not give ear to the accusations brought against the Slavonian teachers. On the contrary, he said that those who maintained that the Gospel should be read in three languages were not right, and they preached a new heresy. When the Pope heard that the brothers were nearing Rome, and that they were bringing the relics of St. Clement, he went out of the city, with all the clergy and a multitude of people, to meet them. Sts. Cyril and Methodius were greatly honored during their stay in Rome. Adrian, the patriarchal bishop of the West, showed them every attention.

The long journey and many hardships in a laborious life told on the health of Cyril. While in Rome his health completely failed him. He understood that his time now had come to its close; therefore, he made preparations, and he wished to take the final vows of an extreme recluse. He awaited the end in calm repose, with a happy conscience. His illness continued for two months. Although he left the world without sorrow, yet the success of the work he had commenced was near to his heart. To Methodius, his brother, he expressed his last will in these touching words: " We two, brother, have been as a contented yoke of oxen, working the same field; and now I fall in the harness, having early finished my day. Thou hast desired the quiet of Mount Olympus, but, I pray thee, leave not the work commenced; for in this labor thy salvation may be secured the sooner." The dying philosopher and pastor for some time continued in prayer, asking for the grace of firm conviction in the faith for all the many people he visited, after which he peacefully gave up his soul to the Lord, at the early age of forty-two years — we might say, on the threshold of complete life of a man, but overcome by labors and sickness. He died on the 14th of February, A. D. 869.

Adrian, the bishop of Rome, with all the prelates and dignitaries of the Western Capital, with a great throng of Christians, carrying lighted candles, attended the funeral of the sainted teacher of the Slavonians, following the holy remains to their place of rest in the Church of St. Clement. Methodius desired to carry the body of his brother to their native country, in accord with the last will of their mother, but the Church of Rome would not consent to it.

St. Methodius returned to the Slavonian countries again to superintend the great work of Christianizing and developing the new literature. Very soon the need of a bishop for the Slavonic people compelled him to return to Rome. This minister of Christ, while spreading the Gospel, endeavored to remain true to the characteristics of a great race, we might say, left to his guardianship, by preserving its history, native culture, and future identity. For this reason he was anxious to obtain letters of authority from the Pope of Rome, who presided in the West, whence came a number of foreign Latin missionaries into his spiritual field. Accordingly St. Methodius was consecrated bishop by the Pope of Rome. Now he came back to his people with power from the West, as St. Cyril had done before, coming from the East, having been consecrated bishop in Constantinople. At this time the Church of Rome was in communion with the Orthodox Church, and this fact proved to be a blessing, coming from the different ancient Apostolic Churches to the young Slavonic Church, insuring her peace and future progress. But by Providence the Slavonic Church was destined to prove her faith in many difficult trials after a little peace. By this time the German war-loving emperors had made their arms felt in southern Europe, and when Rostislav was conquered, in whose stead Sviatopolk gained the ascendency, thanks to the protection of the Germans, the German bishops interfered with the work of St. Methodius in a more arrogant attitude than ever before. They even sought the life of the saint. Prince Kotsel would save him, but in vain. At last, in order to retain for himself the favor of the Germans, Sviatopolk banished Methodius to Shwabia (*i. e.* present Germany). Our apostle was a prisoner for two years, until Pope John VIII., influenced by the example of his predecessor, Adrian, as well as by the constant appeals on the part of the Slavonian Christians, demanded the liberty of Methodius. The Pope went so far as to excommunicate those German bishops who were the cause of the Slavonic teacher's overthrow, until his freedom was secured.

Methodius returned to his Church. It seemed as though he worked now with greater zeal than before. God blessed his efforts for the Gospel. The Slavonians in their contentment prospered not a little. Christian faith, hope, and love was taking a hold on many large provinces. In the mean time, false reports followed one after another to Rome. It must be understood that the new doctrine concerning the procession of the Holy Ghost, which was the cause of the new word *filioque*, that was introduced into the hitherto orthodox creed, had been spread throughout nearly all the churches of the West. Pope John himself did not recognize this innovation. Nevertheless, he sent for St. Methodius on pretext of examining his faith, but in reality it was the Pope's intention to set forth as an example the submission of Methodius and the recognition of papal authority. After questioning him as to the orthodoxy of his teaching, the Pope let him go with a warm commendation. When the enemies of our teachers discovered that they had failed in Rome against him, they now accused St. Methodius before the Emperor of Constantinople, Basil the Macedonian, saying that he was unfaithful to the Orthodox Church, and that he adhered to Rome. The hoary-haired bishop had now to make his way to Constantinople, to defend the work of his glorious brother, and to save their dear Slavonian Church. Our saint's envious intriguers failed again, for he was received with much attention by the emperor and the Patriarch of Constantinople. The patriarch gladly accepted the Slavonic books brought by Methodius;

for he desired to use them in converting the Bulgarians. Once more the people of Pannonia and Moravia were rejoiced to see their beloved pastor. The triumphs of Methodius helped to raise the energy of his disciples, who were continually preaching and translating. Just before the day of St. Demetrius of Salonica, Methodius had completed the translation of the Old Testament, and on the day of the patron saint of his native city he held a grand celebration, all the services being sung in the Slavonic language.

Now the Slavonians from Dalmatia and Croatia to Poland had the privilege of learning the law of God, and hearing His Word, and praising Him in their own tongue. During the sixteen years of his episcopal service, Methodius traveled through all the Slavonian provinces, and, with saintly patience, spread the faith. In Bohemia, for instance, he baptized the Princess Ludmila. While German warriors and Latin monks went through Europe together with fire and sword, St. Methodius labored hard here and there, in small communities, establishing his disciples as teachers and pastors. On another occasion, when the Cheh people, together with their prince, Borivai, of Bohemia, were prepared, they were baptized by Methodius himself.

Sviatopolk, together with the German bishops, by this time feared the great influence of the holy man; but, they waited for his death, in order to persecute his disciples. St. Methodius for several days foretold his own death. He made preparations, and selected a religious and learned man, whose name was Gorazd, to continue the work as his successor. The burial service of the great missionary was held in the Slavonian, Greek, and Latin languages. The loss of their dear teacher was keenly felt by all the people, who wept much. Sviatopolk was about to wreak his vengeance against the disciples of Sts. Cyril and Methodius, when they fled, most of them finding protection and a home in Bulgaria, under King Simeon. From here, they continued to spread enlightenment to many Slavonic countries. They founded schools, and sent out missionaries. Unfortunately, a few provinces, like Poland, for instance, came entirely under the influence of the German bishops and foreign culture. As other Slavonian peoples,

Russia likewise owes much to the translations of Sts. Cyril and Methodius, and also to the work of the disciples of these two great teachers. And Russia, so richly blessed with temporal power and spiritual prosperity, openly acknowledges her sincere gratitude. We also, thank God, have the privilege of praising the blessed names of Cyril and Methodius, who were the beacon-lights of a race whose descendants are now your and our guides in the path of orthodoxy.

ST. SABBAS, THE FIRST ARCHBISHOP OF THE SERVIANS.

January 14.

SABBAS, or Savvo, was born A. D. 1169. He was the youngest son of Stephan Nemanja, who united the Servians in their first kingdom. Leaving his home secretly, he secluded himself, at the age of seventeen years, in the holy Mount Athos. Finally, on being discovered, and yielding to the tears of their son, his parents allowed him to remain there in prayer and study. It was after the death of his father, when the wise Germanus, Patriarch of Constantinople, heard of the holy life of this hermit; and on examining him as to his ability, and consulting with the episcopate of his patriarchate, he desired to consecrate Savvo archbishop for the Servians. But Savvo, in his humility, declined the dignity, and said he was willing to go to his people as a worker, but for an archbishop a better and more qualified man should be sought. However, being prevailed upon by his brothers, the people, and the patriarch, Savvo consented, and he became the first archbishop of the Servian Autocephalous Orthodox Church, which ever since has been in full communion with the Eastern Apostolic Church. St. Savvo's greatest work was the opening of schools, which he multiplied throughout the country. He educated a new choir of faithful clergy, in place of the few Greek missionaries left in the country. It was in 1222 when the apostle of the Servians crowned his brother Dushan as the emperor of the Srbs and Slaveni, his dominion having been spread from the Adriatic to the Black Sea, and from the Danube to the Southern Archipelago. The great and good archbishop fixed a firm foundation for the Orthodox Christian Church in the Balkan country by creating twelve dioceses and consecrating for them twelve Servian bishops.

The holy life of this great Servian, St. Savvo, is attested to by Dositheus of Jerusalem. (See his Twelve Books; see, also, the history of the renowned Shaffarik.) Likewise, many ancient landmarks and hand-written parchments attributed to St. Savvo personally and to his times, may now be seen in the celebrated Mt. Athos and other places. Also several noted Russian authors mention his name and acts. In Greek books of Church service we find hymns which were sung in honor of St. Savvo five hundred years ago.

ST. ALEXANDER NEVSKY.

ALEXANDER is a name well known. We read in history of warriors and statesmen who bear the name. But greater are the saints, who were glorified by God for their virtuous and self-sacrificing life, among whom are also several Alexanders. In the great Russian Empire it is almost impossible to find a family in which some one member is not named Alexander.

Of all the emperors of Russia, the three Alexanders are among the greatest. When you read the life of St. Alexander Nevsky, you will understand why this name is so dear to the Russian.

In the thirteenth century, Russia did not occupy as much country as she does at the present time; Finland belonged to the Swedes, Livonia was ruled over by the Germans; while, to the southwest, the fierce Lithuanians bordered on the Russian provinces. All of these neighbors were at enmity with Russia: the Swedes continually quarreled with the citizens of Novgorod; the Livonian Germans attacked the neighboring provinces, and especially the city of Pskov, with the intention of introducing the Latin religion; and the Lithuanians sacked the towns of the quiet Russians from their side. Besides this, there was no inward peace in Russia, among the different principalities, but more precisely between the ruling dukes. Each province had an independent prince. The most powerful one was the grand duke, or the great prince of Vladimir—the most important city. His influence, being the greatest, was of untold benefit to the kindred Russian tribes, nevertheless the princes quarreled, and seldom gave ear to his counsel. It was at this time that God permitted the horde of Tartars to overrun Russia. These Tartars passed through all Russia, burning and sacking the towns and villages, treading under foot and hoof, meadows and gardens; they took thousands of the inhabitants, together with their wives and children, into captivity; they laid waste the whole land as far as the city of Novgorod.

The neighboring nations, whom we mentioned before, took as an opportunity this misfortune of Russia, and they renewed their attacks from on all sides. The Russian princes were compelled to defend their home against them. Among them was Alexander, the second son of the great prince Yaroslav II. Alexander was born in 1220; from his childhood, he was distinguished by his understanding, meekness, wisdom, and piety. He knew how to fulfill his duty sacredly, and deserve the love of the people. God who helped him in life, also glorified him by miracles after he passed into eternity. Devastating the land of the Russians, the Tartars went south, and occupied the steppes along the rivers Dnieper, Volga, and Ural, as far as the Black and Caspian Seas. Here Batee set up his golden horde, or empire, and built the city known as Sarai, not far from the mouth of the Volga. Henceforth the Russian princes must pay tribute to the Tartars. Batee, the new dictator of Russia, confirmed Yaroslav II (Vsevolodovicha) as great prince of Vladimir; Alexander was given him the country of Novgorod, which had remained free and unharmed by the Tartars.

Although Novgorod was not spoiled by the touch of the Tartars, still it suffered misfortune of another kind. Great fires destroyed churches and houses, and defaced whole streets of the city. From droughts and the failure of crops the inhabitants often suffered terrible hunger, as a result from which epidemic diseases also mutilated the populace. The Germans and Lithuanians were prepared to fall upon Novgorod any day. Having become the prince of Novgorod, Alexander endeavored to shield his people from misfortune and their enemies. He took care that the judges ruled their courts with justice; he taught the inhabitants to live in peace and help the poor; he built posts on the frontier for their defense against the Germans and Lithuanians. In the mean time the King of Sweden gathered a large force, which he sent on barges to the river Neva, under the command of his kinsman, Birger. The daring general, hoping to take Novgorod, sent the prince word: " Come against me, if thou art courageous." The people were stricken with fear; they could not count on their small force against so numerous an enemy; but Alexander put his trust in God, and the justice of his cause inspired him with courage. He prayed earnestly in the church of St. Sophia, received the bishop's blessing, and then cheerfully exclaimed as he set out with his men: "We are not many, and the enemy is strong; but the power of God is not in numbers, it is in the right."

At night they came near to the banks of the Neva, to the place upon which the city of St. Petersburg was built later, and here they camped for the night. In the morning, a warrior approached Alexander, and told him that, as he stood on watch during the night, in view of the sea, toward morning—when the sun was rising—he suddenly heard a loud voice come from the sea, and on turning in that direction, he saw a ship sailing; upon the deck of the ship he saw the holy martyrs, Boris and Gleb, who held each other in embrace while conversing; he heard St. Boris say: "Brother Gleb, let us go quickly to the help of our kinsman Alexander; a great danger threatens him." After these words, the holy brothers and the ship disappeared.

This vision raised the spirit of the soldiers. About noontime Alexander met the Swedes on the banks of the Neva. The battle was a long one. Alexander, personally, brought down Birger, with a spear, and toward evening, completely overcame the foe, who took to his ships and passed over to his own land, but not until after leaving many dead comrades. For this victory the people gave Alexander the name of *Nevsky*.

Alexander returned to Novgorod in triumph; but here a greater trouble awaited him. The Novgorodans revolted against their prince. Offended by their unfaithfulness, Alexander did not wish to remain any longer with them; and, taking his family and property, he went to Suzdal, his native place. As soon as the Lithuanians and Germans heard of Alexander's departure, they fell upon the Novgorod and Pskov countries. Then it was that the Novgorodans thought of their behavior; they repented and sent their bishop to solicit Alexander's pardon, and to petition him to return and deliver them from their enemy. Alexander had forgotten the wrong done him; he summoned his field companions, and came to Novgorod, from which the intruders fled.

But the Germans did not give up their pretensions. After some time, they again raised an army to march on Novgorod. This time they had in their long columns many Germans, who came to them upon invitation from their native land. Their legions were many times greater than Alexander's company; nevertheless, the brave prince sallied forth, and met the Germans on the ice of Lake Chindckoe, where he dealt them a severe blow. Many were slain on the enemy's side, and many more were captured. This encounter is known as the "Ice Battle." Still the Lithuanians and Germans continued to assault the Russians, and each time Alexander conquered or drove them away. God visibly helped the strictly religious prince.

In the mean time, Alexander's father (Yaroslav, the great prince of Vladimir), died while he was returning home from the Tartars' horde. The Chan appointed his brother to succeed him, *i. e.* Sviatoslav, uncle to Alexander. But it was not long before the younger brothers of Alexander began to quarrel with the great prince, with the view of obtaining the throne of the province of Vladimir. Alexander advised them to decide the case by the Chan's judgment. The princes agreed, and Alexander, with his younger brother, Andrew, went to the Tartars. They first came to the Golden Horde; but from here they were obliged to travel beyond the Volga, to the steppes of Mongolia, where Mengoo, himself, was reigning, to whom even Batee was subjected. After a long journey, the two princes came back again. Andrew was appointed great prince of Vladimir, and Alexander of Kiev. Sviatoslav, the old uncle, must, against his will, give the country of Vladimir to Andrew, yet he never made peace with him. He tried by all means to regain the throne of the great prince. With this intention, he reported to the Chan that Andrew was not faithful, and that he did not obey the Chan's orders. The Tartars sent a numerous band of barbarians. Andrew met it with his force, but he was repulsed with great loss, and he himself fled to the Germans. The province of Vladimir was trampled over and robbed. Alexander knew that the Chan would punish all Russia for Andrew's behavior. To save his people and their homes, he went to the capital of the horde to intercede for Andrew and the whole land of Russia.

The Chan received Alexander graciously, and appointed him great prince of Vladimir, Kiev, and Novgorod.

Having ascended the throne of Vladimir, Alexander's labor and cares multiplied. Now he became the only defender of the orthodox faith, and the people before the Tartars. He was obliged to act with patience and submission, but not with saber in hand. He understood that his force could not withstand the great bands of Tartars, and that each opposition would bring greater trouble upon the people. Alexander was great prince for eleven years, and in that time, he succeeded in doing much good, both for the Church and the people. On his petition, the clergy, as the servants of God, were freed from paying tax to the horde; he also obtained a grant by which he could install an orthodox bishop in the capital of the Tartar Empire itself. Alexander gained for the Christian religion the respect of the Tartars.

One of his greatest cares was to relieve the inhabitants somewhat in their tax-payments, and save them from poverty. Having conquered Russia, the Tartars left her to the rule of Russian princes, while they only demanded tribute. The people of Novgorod caused Alexander much anxiety. With great difficulty, he scarcely dissuaded them on several occasions from sending back and even killing the tax-collectors. He was mindful of the evil which endangered the whole land of Russia.

The prince was to accomplish one more laborious task; and it was his last. The Tartars took into their service, the Chozars, and sent them out as revenue assessors. These new collectors were more avaricious than the former ones; they spared no one, and they were also disrespectful before the altars and holy places. The people bore this for a long time, but at last they lost their patience. Such cities as Vladimir, Suzdal, Rostov, arose and destroyed their oppressors. Already great legions in the horde were preparing for the punishment of the disobedient. The great prince set out to journey to the horde. He decided to die for his country, or save it. God blessed with success this last undertaking of Alexander, and the Russian provinces were freed from another overrunning of Tartars.

Returning from the chief camp or capital of the Tartars, Alexander became ill on reaching the town of Gorodets, on the Volga (in the province of Nijni-Novgorod), and perceiving that his end was not far off, he desired to be tonsured a monk. Upon taking the vows, the name *Alexis* was given him. The dying prince called to his bedside the princes that could be summoned from the neighborhood, the noblemen who accompanied him on his journey, and a number of the people, and spoke to them of his last wishes; then blessing all present, he forgave all every offense, and asked in return to be forgiven himself. After this, he confessed before the priest, and partook of the holy mysteries, dying soon after, on the 14th of November, 1263, being about 44 years of age.

The inhabitants of Gorodets wept over the body of the holy prince. As yet no information of this event reached Vladimir. St. Kirill (Cyril) only, the metropolitan of Vladimir, during the church service felt a heavy sadness oppress his soul, and turning to the people said: "The Russian nation's sun has set." No one understood his words. Then his eyes streaming with tears, he said: "The great prince, Alexander, is now dead."

The funeral procession moved from Gorodets to Vladimir. The metropolitan and the people met with it at a distance of ten versts from the city. It was a sad, weeping multitude. The burial service was held in the cathedral, after which the body was lain to rest in the large church of the monastery of Our Blessed Lady. The glory of the miracles of St. Alexander spread from hence throughout all Russia. Many sick and crippled ones came to his tomb, and were healed. During the reign of the Emperor, Peter the Great, the relics of St. Alexander were brought to St. Petersburg, on the banks of the Neva, and placed in the Alexandro-Nevskaia Lavra, which was erected to his honor, and where they lie to the present day. The Church celebrates St. Alexander Nevsky Day, on the 23d of November, and also keeps the memory of the day when his holy remains were carried from Vladimir, to St. Petersburg, which is the 30th of August.

THE LIFE OF ST. PHILIP, METROPOLITAN OF MOSCOW.

January 9.

SAINT PHILIP came from an ancient noble family known by the name of Kolitchev. His own name while in the world was Theodore. He was born in Moscow, in the year 1507, and, after receiving a good education, he was appointed to a position in the imperial service. High honors awaited the fortunately established young nobleman; moreover, he was a favorite with John, the Grand Duke, who was still in his minority. But Theodore was not taken by earthly grandeur; for early in life he aspired to live for God alone. Once, when attending the public worship of the Church, his whole being, we might say, was penetrated with the power of the Holy Ghost on hearing these words of the Holy Gospel: *No man can serve two masters:*

for either he will hate the one, and love the other; or else he will hold to one, and despise the other. (Matt. vi: 24.) He resolved that he would not serve the world and riches, but leave all and enter the Solovetsky monastery, on the islands of the White Sea, in the north of Russia, which especially attracted him by its distance and severity of rule.

Theodore was about thirty years of age when he carried out his intention. He went on his journey empty-handed. Because of insufficient means, and being wearisome of the road, he was compelled to stop on the way for a while, and hire himself out as a workman. Having earned some money, he continued his journey, and finally reached the Solovetsky convent.

The aged abbot, whose name was Alexis, received him kindly, and made him a beginner. Without complaining, Theodore eagerly did all that was required of him; he carried water, cut wood, worked in the kitchen, in the garden, and in the mill. He meekly served all; he sometimes suffered sharp words, and was even beaten; yet he bore all patiently. It might appear that such a life was a difficult one for the son of a rich nobleman who was brought up in all comfort; but the desire to please God by labor and obedience conquered all. Theodore did not lose courage in the tiresome undertaking. A year and a half thus had passed, when the superior tonsured him, giving the new monk the name of Philip.

After a few years it became evident that Philip was capable in all the branches of work in a large monastery, and he was esteemed as a worthy and pious monk. The abbot Alexis was old, and he desired to be retired in favor of St. Philip. But Philip would not hear of it. It was after the whole brotherhood unanimously elected and entreated him to become their superior, that Philip consented to be elevated to the abbotship; still he would not take into his hands alone the rule, while Father Alexis lived.

When Philip came to Novgorod to be ordained by the bishop of that city, some circumstances disclosed the fact that he belonged to the well-known family of Moscow.

As a superior, the abbot Philip ruled with a firm hand, yet with discretion and love. He enforced discipline, but he was the first to set the good example. The monastery was a poor one, while the brotherhood increased in numbers by new-comers, and it became difficult to maintain them, notwithstanding the few simple wants of the monks. By this time St. Philip came into possession of his ancestral inheritance. He spent it in renovating and enlarging the monastery; he built churches which were more secure and warmer for the brethren on those sea islands in the extreme north. Besides this, he exerted himself and obtained from the emperor himself grants of valuable land situated on the mainland. Now Philip invented and introduced new industries for the support of his monks, and likewise for the prosperity of the surrounding settlements with their inhabitants.

In the mean time John, the Grand Duke, had come to the throne. On two occasions, important in the history of both the Russian Church and Empire, the Emperor John sent for Philip to be present in Moscow, and lend his counsel. After each return, Philip brought good tidings from Moscow which were full of encouragement for the future of the state and

John's reign. However, the following course of events, brought about a fearful change.

In the midst of his building schemes and quiet work among the praying brethren of the distant north, St. Philip received a sudden order from John the Terrible, as the king was by this time known, to come at once to Moscow and occupy the Archiepiscopal-Metropolitan chair. To leave the holy abode where he had lived for eighteen years was not an easy thing for Philip to do; moreover, he felt that he was going to a very thorny labor. Everything had changed since he was in the capital. The fact that the spiritual confessor of the Terrible John, a priest by the name of Sylvester, was banished and confined in this same Solovetsky monastery was itself a loud witness as to the nature of daily occurrences. It now seemed as though it was an impossibility to speak the truth in the face of the ruler.

In order to explain his relations with Philip, we must briefly review the history of John. He was but three years old, when, after the death of his father, he came to the throne of Russia. It was not long either before John had lost his mother also. His relations, together with the foremost nobility, did not fulfill their duty toward the royal child; *i. e.* they were careless, and did not educate him in the strict rules of virtue; but they indulged his whims, letting him have all, as his own inclination swayed to, thinking thereby to be favored by him when he would be the independent ruler. Having reached the seventeenth year of his age, John proclaimed himself of age, and the independent sovereign; he discharged his guardians, putting some of them to death, and abandoned himself to wild passions. This was a grievous time for Russia. It was a pastime for John to witness the most fearful sufferings; his own pleasure was the paramount consideration. The sufferings of the population were greatly added to by a fire which almost entirely destroyed Moscow. Many people were lost, and a larger number were bereft of all their belongings. John, in his anger, sought for the offenders, when suddenly a priest came before him, whose name was Sylvester. Pointing to the city enveloped in flames, he fearlessly announced that the emperor himself was the cause of all the misfortune; that God punished them with calamities, for the severe and unrighteous government. The words of truth, which reached John so seldom, made a strong impression upon him. He acknowledged his guilt, shed tears of repentance, prayed God for forgiveness and help, and firmly resolved to correct himself. After some days, having first received the Holy Communion, John called the people to assemble in the square. Bowing on all sides, he asked to be forgiven for the past, and promised that in the future he would care for the happiness of his subjects, and that he would govern them with love and justice.

Thus for thirteen years the Russians enjoyed prosperity; and John greatly widened the confines of his empire by successful conquests. But a change took place. John, tired of the good advice of Father Sylvester, and his counselor, by the name of Adashev. At this time the good empress died, the virtuous Anastasia, who strongly influenced John for good. The sovereign became dejected; again his evil mood led him to be wicked. He banished Sylvester and Adashev, declaring that they infringed upon his freedom. John soon found excuses for breaking the rules of morality. He surrounded himself by flatterers. Each day he became more ferocious; and he fully deserved the epithet of *Terrible*, as he is known in history.

As John became more dark and suspicious, he continually accused his subjects of treason against him; and so he formed a bodyguard, in whom he put all his confidence. These men, John called his *Opritchina* (select), while every other class of people not belonging to it, was termed the *Zemshtchina* (belonging to the land or country). The Opritchniki were at liberty to do as they pleased. The Zemshtchina were at the mercy of men who had no respect for the law, and no conception of morality. The Opritchniki murdered people without the fear of prosecution. This is the condition in which Russia was at the time that Philip, the abbot of the Solovetsky Monastery, was summoned by John to be appointed Metropolitan.

The brothers of Solovetsky, with sorrow, bid farewell to St. Philip. On his way the citizens of Novgorod tendered him a reception and begged him to be their advocate with the emperor, whose vengeance they feared, as they had fallen under the ban of John the Terrible. In Moscow, all trembled before the *Opritchina*. Philip resolved to tell the sovereign the whole truth, though he would be obliged to sacrifice his life for it. Having arrived in Moscow, his first care was to obtain the co-operation of the bishops; but even they feared the penalty for opposing the evil will of the sovereign. "Your silence allows the emperor to fall into sin," said he to them; "and by not speaking, you lose your own soul, for you prefer the vanishing glory of the world and your safety, and not the fulfillment of your duties."

While persuading Philip to accept the archbishop's chair in the imperial capital, John often quoted words of the Holy Scriptures, for he was one of those kind of men who think they can only by the use of words and outward signs of religion, even fastings and nightly prostrations, obtain the grace of God, which is a power communicated to the heart regenerated. But John did not repent sincerely; he was not truly humble before God, and his prayer was unfruitful.

St. Philip was horrified when he saw the

sovereign, for he remembered him, a man beautiful to behold. Now, his face was marked with lines of dissipation; his hair turned gray before the time; cruelty and sin were expressed in his features; he was hideous.

Philip began to persuade the ruler that he might disband the Opritchina; he explained to him all the evil which it brought upon Russia. He even refused to become Metropolitan, if John would not destroy the Opritchina. "O sire!" said he, in conclusion, "I once knew thee as a pious defender of the truth, and a successful ruler of your country. Believe me, even now, no one thinks aught against thee; put away the cause of offense, and hold to your former piety. The Lord himself had told us, *If a kingdom be divided in itself, it will come to naught.* Christ, our common Master, bids us love one another; the whole law is included in the love to God and our neighbor."

John listened with apparent attention to the words of Philip, but they had not the desired effect. He would not give up his Opritchina, and demanded that Philip without any conditions accept the office of Metropolitan. The hope that he might be of use to his fatherland moved Philip to submit, and he was compelled to sign a promise that he would not meddle with the affairs of the court and the Opritchina. Accordingly, Philip was consecrated bishop, and installed Metropolitan of Moscow on the 25th of July, 1566.

Quiet reigned for a very short time. Naturally, the wicked Opritchniks feared Philip's influence over the emperor; and, they endeavored by all means to injure him. John was not successful in his Livonian campaign, and he returned angry and downcast. One of Philip's relations took part in a diplomatical consultation with the king of Poland, which failed; of course, this incident was treasured as evidence against the Metropolitan by his enemies. At the same time the Opritchniks accused many of the higher nobility, whose estates consequently were confiscated. Suspicion easily entered the dark soul of John; again persecution and torture hunted down many an innocent one; blood flowed in streams; the population was panic-stricken. Philip resolved to approach the sovereign with a bitter exhortation.

John became impatient. When he had seen that Philip was in earnest, and feared not his anger, John departed in a rage. The time was now gone when the words of truth could awaken repentance in the soul of John. He hardened his heart against all that was good, and truthful reprimands only aroused his anger. But St. Philip in fulfilling his holy duty, and in order to save John, was prepared to die for it, if needs be.

Once, on a Sunday, when St. Philip offered the liturgy in the cathedral of the Blessed Repose of Our Lady, John came into the temple with a crowd of Opritchniki at the end of the service. John had on a black habit, such as monks wear, while his drunken followers were dressed also in different unbecoming apparel. The emperor stood close to the Metropolitan and waited for his blessing: but the archbishop kept his gaze upon a sacred picture, as though he did not see or recognize John. At this, one of John's favorites said: "Holy father, the sovereign asks for your blessing."

Philip then looked upon John, and said; "I do not recognize the Tsar in this strange dress, nor do I recognize him in the acts of government. O sire! we offer here the unbloody sacrifice, but over against the altar flows the innocent blood of Christians. Even the heathen have laws, justice, and mercy, but there is none in Russia. The property and life of citizens have no protection; robbery and murder are committed in the name of the ruler. Thou art elevated upon a throne, but there is one who is the Most High, our common Judge! How wilt thou appear at the trial before Him, stained as thou art with the blood of thy subjects? Sire! as a pastor of souls, I say to thee, fear God!"

John became wild with anger; he heavily struck the floor with his staff and cried out: "Thou black-hood [*i. e.* monk] is it our power that thou wouldst contradict? We shall see thy strength!"

Life with its circumstances went on from bad to worse. The country was filled with iniquity and fear. Now the Opritchnina were set on putting Philip out of their way. During a holy day, in the midst of the service, they made their way into the cathedral, and, dragging the old Metropolitan from the altar, they tore away from his shoulders the sacred vestments, and putting a ragged cassock upon him, they drove him out of the holy temple. The enemies of St. Philip, after much endeavoring, found a monk, a certain Paisius, who—partly bought, and partly out of a sinful fear—agreed to be a witness against the archbishop. The Tsar called a council of bishops, and he himself sat in their midst, as the presiding judge of the pseudo-ecclesiastical court. The bishops feared to defend Philip. Only one, German, the Bishop of Kazan, raised his voice, declaring the innocence of Philip. Even John dared not to sentence Philip to death at once; but he gave orders that the Opritchniki take him to prison, knowing well that his evil companions would carry out his secret desire, and sooner or later murder Philip. And truly the tortures that they put him to are too numerous and horrible to be repeated. The saint, who had accustomed himself to a strict and severe life from his youth, with patience bore all suffering, and by God's grace remained alive. After his imprisonment he was transferred from monastery to monastery, by order of John, who was afraid of the multitudes that gathered from all parts to receive the blessing of the aged bishop.

Philip continued to bear his unbearable life. John tortured and put to death his relations in the mean time. A year had thus gone by. Now Philip was kept under a rough guard in a monastery of Tver. At this time John the Terrible was passing by Tver on his way to Novgorod, in order to wreak his vengeance on a number of citizens there. He did not forget Philip. He sent one Maliuta Skooratov to the monastery in which the Metropolitan was confined. St. Philip had foreseen that his end was near, for in the morning of this same day he partook of the Holy Communion. He was praying when the bandit entered his cell. "Holy father, give the Tsar a blessing for his journey to Novgorod," said the Opritchnik. "Only the good obtain blessings for good purposes," answered Philip; "but go about your work, wherefor you have been sent; do not deceive me by asking for God's gift." Then Philip exclaimed: "O Almighty Lord, receive my spirit!" Skooratov threw himself upon the prelate, and choked him. When he had committed the crime, he coolly walked out and informed the superior and monks that Philip had died from a stroke of paralysis, and that he should be buried at once. This happened on the 23d of December, 1570.

Twenty years after the death of St. Philip, during the reign of Theodore, the good son of John the Terrible, the brethren of the Solovetsky monastery petitioned the Tsar to be allowed to carry the body of their beloved abbot to their home in the far north. This was granted, and when they opened the grave in order to remove the remains, they found the whole body of St. Philip in a perfect state of preservation. It was a fete day in the Solovetsky monastery, when the holy relics arrived there. Many wonderful cures were effected at the casket of the prelate. In 1640, in the time of Alexis Michaelovich, Philip was proclaimed by the church as a saint of God, in whose memory a certain day was set aside in the calendar. In 1652 the relics of St. Philip were brought to Moscow. Nikon, the Metropolitan of Novgorod, himself sailed to the Solovetsky convent, and informed the superior with the brethren, that it was the will of the Tsar "to bring the relics of St.

Philip to the imperial city, that he again may be installed in his diocese, and that by his coming he may absolve the sin of his ancestor, the Tsar John." The transfer of the holy relics of the Metropolitan is commemorated on the 3d of July.

Up to this day there can be seen in the Moscow Cathedral of the Blessed Repose of Our Lady the remains of the holy martyr, who zealously fulfilled the different duties required of him; who set an example of obedience and humbleness by his monastic life; an example of untiring energy during his abbotship, undaunted courage in his relations with John, and a Christian patience in suffering.

WHY

ORTHODOX CHRISTIANS AT DIVINE LITURGY BRING BREAD LOAVES, AND THE PARTICLES, WHICH ARE CUT OUT FROM THEM, ARE OFFERED FOR THE LIVING AND DEAD, AND THE MEANING OF THIS RITE.

IN the Orthodox Church there is a religious and salutary custom, which we, unfortunately, seldom see practiced in this country.

When you go to Holy Liturgy, for instance, in the churches throughout the broad land of Russia, you cannot help observing how the faithful eagerly enter, and there, by the church doors, buy a church loaf, or two, have it (or them), brought into the sanctuary, together with a paper (or a small blank-book) upon which some names are written; then, after particles have been cut out from these breads, they take them again, and on leaving the church, they bring the loaves home with them.

During the great holy days, and on the days when the dead are remembered, also during Lent when a great many people receive the holy sacraments of Christ, a large number of these church breads are brought into the sanctuary. An especially large quantity of loaves are brought during the year by the faithful in those temples to which thousands of pilgrims flock in order to offer their devotion to the holy relics, to the holy icona of the Lord, the Mother of God, and to the saints of God. Having received back their *prosphora*, or loaf, after a particle had been taken from it in the sanctuary, the faithful carefully handle it, and, crossing themselves, kiss it; then, after the Liturgy, they carry it to their homes, and here, with all the members of the household, they eat it before they partake of their regular meal, *i. e.* upon an empty stomach.

This custom is hardly ever practiced in this country among our Orthodox Christians, and yet this ceremony is an ancient and religious act; it is very important and salutary. That it is really such, we will now consider.

Let us, first of all, mention the fact that five bread loaves are used in offering the Divine Liturgy in the Orthodox Church. From the first one a conveniently large piece is cut and put on the paten, which at first is a representation of the Lord Jesus Christ; and after, during the hymn, *Thee we sing, Thee we bless*, it is transubstantiated (*i. e.* mystically changed) into the true Body of Christ. Even so does the wine with water which was poured into the chalice during the offertory or first part of the Liturgy, become at the same time the real and life-giving Blood of the Lord. This larger particle is therefore called the Holy Lamb.

From the second *prosphora* a particle is taken and put on the paten to the right side of the Holy Lamb, " in honor and in remembrance of the Most Blessed Lady and Mother of God."

From out the third loaf nine particles are cut and put to the left of the Holy Lamb on the paten, in honor and in remembrance of the nine orders of saints.

From the fourth one (*i. e., prosphora,* which is a Greek word, and means *offering*) several particles are taken and put before the Holy Lamb, for the health and salvation of the living.

First of all, the priest makes mention of the

Orthodox Patriarchs, the Most Holy Synod, the bishop of his diocese, with all the clergy, and then lays down upon the paten a particle; after this another, when he mentions the name of his sovereign, the whole of the royal house, and finally he names others and all the living, and those by name who asked to be remembered. At each name, the priest takes a small particle and puts it down before the Lamb.

From the fifth loaf particles are cut out and put on the paten in remembrance and for the forgiveness of the sins of all the departed, commencing with the patriarchs and kings. The priest makes mention of each departed one whom he wishes or whom he has been requested to mention by name, and for each he places a bit of the loaf before the Holy Lamb.

In this manner parts are taken from the five breads, which are necessary in offering the Divine Liturgy.

What is done with those loaves which the faithful bring, and why are they brought?

From these also particles are taken for the living and the dead. Their names are read (from each family's book or list), and the priest cuts out a particle for the health and salvation of each one, if the name be of those among the living, or for the remembrance and forgiveness of the sins of one, if the name be of those among the departed. All these particles must be put on the paten together with those taken from the fourth and fifth loaves.

In this manner in the beginning of the Liturgy a great many particles lie upon the paten around the principal part or bread, *i. e.* the Holy Lamb. These particles represent the souls of the saints and all the Orthodox, in whose name they were put there. When during the singing—*Thee we hymn, Thee we bless*—the principal part, which was taken from the first bread, becomes transmuted into the Real Body of Christ, and the wine in the cup becomes the Very Blood of Christ; then it is plainly understood, that from that moment the particles lying upon the paten, and the souls of the people whom they represent, do stand before the Lord Jesus Christ Himself, invisibly and mystically present upon the holy table in the holy sacrament. Finally, after the clergy and laity partake of the Holy Communion, all the particles are put from off the paten into the chalice, and they absorb of the Life-giving Blood of Christ; consequently the souls of the living and the dead are brought into a mutual, gracious communion with the Lord Jesus Christ.

To the spiritual view of all standing and praying in the temple at that time, the following should be pictured: Upon the heavenly throne He, the Lord Jesus Christ Himself, is seated, our Redeemer and Saviour, and before Him stand: the Most Holy Mother of God, " ever constant in prayer" before Her Son and God for the whole race of mankind; then all the saints, also our intercessors and mediators; and all the living and the departed of the faithful, in whose names parts have been set aside, who are expecting from the Lord for themselves, through the prayers of the Mother of God, all the saints, and all the believing, mercy, forgiveness of sins, and eternal salvation. At that moment to all before the Lamb the saving grace of God is communicated from the throne. When the particles absorb of the Life-giving Blood, at the time the priest prays: *Wash, O Lord, the sins of all those mentioned here by Thy precious Blood, and the prayers of*

Thy saints, the souls, which are represented by the particles, are brought into a mutual communion with the Lord Redeemer, and thereby the saints of God obtain a greater glory and happiness in heaven, while the living and the dead, washed in the most Precious Blood of the Son of God, receive the forgiveness of sins and inherit life eternal.

II.

The significance of the particle taken out by the priest for some one of our relatives or acquaintance is such. The soul of the one mentioned appears before the throne of God and prays to the Lord in devout fear, and its prayer, strengthened by the intercessions of the prayers of all the blessed in heaven, and the earnest prayer of all the faithful present, especially of those who brought the loaf and asked for the prayers of a priest, and also by the prayers of him who offers the sacrament, *i. e.* the priest, such a prayer of the soul becomes efficient and powerful. The Lord mercifully accepts such a prayer of the soul. Sinners themselves have appeared from the other world, and revealed to their relatives how great a relief they have experienced in their condition beyond the grave after the Divine Liturgy has been offered upon earth, in which a particle was set aside *in remembrance and for the forgiveness of their sins.*

And the living? The living also receive forgiveness of sins, and by this all *that which is necessary for life and piety.*

Our offering of loaves in the temple of the Lord, so that particles may be cut from them, is of much importance for ourselves likewise.

And for ourselves we must pray and put before the Lamb a particle of the bread. The priest at the offertory must put upon the paten a particle for himself also, at the same time praying in these words: *Be mindful, O Lord, of me an unworthy one, and forgive me all sins, voluntary and involuntary.* We should each one of us put our own names in the "book of remembrance," so that the priest may take out a particle for us also, and thereby move in prayer for us the whole Church, so that, when we stand before the face of the Lord, we may enter into a gracious communion with Him at the time our particle, together with the others, becomes immersed during the Liturgy in the Life-giving Blood of the Son of God.

Besides this, a *prosphora* is brought into the temple as an offering to God. Any gift of ours, any sacrifice of ours is pleasing to God when it expresses our gratefulness, our love to God, from whom we ourselves receive *every good and perfect gift*. On coming into the Church we buy and light before an holy icona a candle. This is our offering to God, and it shows that we came into the temple—the place of God's habitation, to pray as constantly and fervently, as brightly and warmly as our candle burns before the holy icona. The *prosphora*, which we buy and give into the sanctuary that particles be taken from it, though it is returned to us, yet it is our gift to God also, which testifies to our desire to pray with greater zeal for ourselves and for those who are dear to our hearts. This little gift of ours reminds us of Christian custom in the early days of Christ's Church. At that time all the faithful, when they came to church for Holy Liturgy, brought bread and wine. From all that was brought, the priest selected what was necessary for the sacrament, and the remaining bread and wine was divided after the Liturgy among all those present. A brotherly table was spread, which showed that the faithful lived in love and close communion.

Now we offer only a small loaf in the Church; yet this bread is our gift to God, our offering to the Divine Liturgy, wherefore the very name of it is *prosphora*, which in the Greek language means *offering*. From it is taken but a small, necessary particle for our communication with the Grace of God, while nearly the entire loaf is returned to us from the altar, which we for our sanctification eat with thanksgiving.

As a gift of God, brought to the holy table, which was used in taking the particles which have such an important signification, then given to us as a blessing and for our sanctification by partaking of it,—the *prosphora* should be received as a bread blessed, with appropriate religious consideration. Hereby is explained the custom for taking back again the loaf from the sanctuary, making the sign of the cross upon one's self, and kissing it, after the service carefully bringing it home, and dividing it among the members of the family, to be eaten before other food. Below is an incident told in the life of St. Zosima—the wonder-worker. St. Zosima once gave to a merchant a *prosphora* as a blessing, but the merchant on his way home carelessly dropped it. A dog running up was about to eat the bread, but each time, when it was about to take it, a flame came forth from out the *prosphora* and kept it back. A monk of the Solovetsky Monastery saw this (his name was Makarius); he drove away the dog; devoutly crossing himself, he took the loaf and brought it to St. Zosima, who recognized the *prosphora* given by him to the merchant. And so the church loaf is holy bread, and we should handle it carefully and devoutly.

Such, then, is the significance of the *prosphora*, which we offer in church. Therefore, who desires for self, or one's relatives, and for acquaintance, health and salvation, and for the departed forgiveness of sins and the kingdom of heaven; let such a one earnestly pray to God, especially during the Liturgy, and not neglect, on account of carelessness, to bring into the church a *prosphora*, let such a one not begrudge a few cents for the loaf. When the priest takes from the loaf particles, for the one who brought it, and for those who are mentioned in the book of remembrance brought with it, and puts the particles on the paten before the face of the Lord, so that they may after absorb the Life-giving Blood of the Lord, such a prayer then must be more real and profitable, as for the one who brought the offering, likewise also for those in whose name or memory prayers may be asked for. When this loaf is brought home and eaten, thereby such a person with his or her family partake of the blessing of God.

ADDRESS

Delivered in the Presence of His Right Reverence Nicholas, Bishop of Alaska and the Aleutian Islands, the Members and Friends of the Orthodox Church and the Parish School of St. Sergius, in San Francisco.

AS I stand here in the midst of this gathering, I picture in my mind another company, greater than this, filling the spacious halls of a more magnificent structure in the capital city of the Russian Empire—*Matushka Moskva* (dear mother Moscow). My imagination reaches still farther out, and I behold another throng of busy citizens, together with young Seminarians and prayerfully inclined Christians, away off in Siberia, in the city of Irkoutsk. Methinks I hear them speak the very name of him whom they have come to honor, *Innocentius*. My whole being thrills with a veneration at the sound of that name. My heart is filled with gladness when I think of the pure joy and reasonable pride of the country folk in rural Anginskoe of the Province of Irkoutsk—the native home of the Most Reverend Metropolitan Innocent.

Yet all these multitudes and territorial distance are but a part of the whole, celebrating a great event. Look you, the tribes of Kamchatka with the Yakout race sing of him, while the Aleut and the Alaskan Indians gratefully commemorate their teacher on this day—the one hundredth anniversary of his birth. While the great Orthodox Missionary Society in Russia, which to-day upholds our prosperous Church in Japan and in other parts of the world, is paying honor to the sacred memory of its founder, we too bless this one hundredth birthday of our first Bishop in America—the same Innocentius, Metropolitan of Moscow.

This great Missionary, who passed away from this visible world eighteen years ago, and rests with his remains in the holy Troitse Sergiev Monastery, still dwells in the loving hearts of the different peoples of his spiritual charge. I understand and feel the special privilege which I enjoy to-night, and for which I most heartily thank thee, Gracious Bishop and Most Reverend Father in God. Deeply feeling the love of our Archpastors, I become bold and venture to look into the unseen, where I behold the spiritual eyes of our first hard-working Missionary, with kindly light beaming upon this gathering and approving of the feeble words of your son (to the Bishop), and your brother (to the Clergy), and your pastor (to the Congregation)—one of the first born of the young American Orthodox Church!

John Veniaminov, indeed, was a great man. As one of the first priests in Alaska, he labored for fifteen long years in several parts of that vast region, making his home, principally, first in Ounalashka and then in Sitkha. In those pioneer days of Alaska an Aleutian badairka or small canoe made of the skin of a walrus was the only means he had for his constant locomotion, and not seldom for his voyages of a longer course. It often happened that, in a mean, wet climate, his only comfort for whole months would be found in an earthen dug-out. I will not detain you by repeating; you will soon hear, and also read for yourselves, of his life, and then you will know how in the Providence of God the Reverend Father John became to be known by the name of Innocent, and how he returned to Alaska—as the first bishop there, and likewise our first bishop in America! Brief accounts of his life are now printed in English, as well as in Russian and other languages, and may be had for nothing, comparatively.

There are several people in this city who have personally seen him, and remember well the wholesome instructions of their gentle pastor—Bishop Innocent, later the Metropolitan of Moscow. Besides the elder brethren and the elder sisters among you, some of the people mentioned are also fathers in their community. Our present Bishop and beloved Father in God was at one time under the spiritual rule of the Most Reverend Innocentius, and that was during his student life in the Academy of Moscow, when Innocent was the Bishop of the Church of God in that Province.

I have strong reasons for maintaining my assertion that this Missionary Priest, John Veniaminov, also landed on our shores here, and—how I love to dwell on the thought!—he bestowed God's blessing upon our beautiful California. It was in the fall of 1838 that this God-fearing worker left Sitkha in a sailing vessel—to voyage down the whole length of the great Pacific, and make his way around Cape Horn to Europe and St. Petersburg. At that time the government of Alaska, following the wise counsel of Baranov (another great man), obtained and held land in California, where it had a flourishing colony in the part now known as Sonoma county. Baranov was well aware of the worth of Alaska, but he needed California as a storehouse of grain for the Great North with its many resources and grand coast. The globe-circumnavigating vessels, coming from the north, certainly must have anchored in California waters, in order to take on supplies and make a final preparation before setting sail to round the Cape for Europe. And so it is possible that our dear Missionary may have even offered the Divine Liturgy in the chapel at Fort Ross, and also baptized the Indians in Russian River. I do not attempt to speculate on the idea that our apostle trod the sands where now our splendid city of San Francisco is built. For memory's sake I simply ask: Is there not a history attached to Russian Hill in San Francisco?

A most remarkable man was this Russian priest from Siberia. He was a mechanic, navigator, school-teacher, administrator, and a preacher of the Gospel. A poor orphaned boy, too young to earn his own bread, must depend upon the charity of poor relatives and even strangers for his very existence. From a little town in the heart of Siberia he finds his way into the city of Irkoutsk, where he becomes a pastor, beloved by his devoted people. Then he goes, as he thought, to give up himself with his entire strength and knowledge to the simple Aleuts, *who sat in darkness* in the distant islands of the ocean. It was he, as he afterwards sat in the councils of the Most Holy Governing Synod of our Church, who moved the proposition that the Orthodox Bishop in America should transfer his residence from Sitkha to San Francisco.

God selected the priest, John Veniaminov, to bear the light of Orthodox Christianity from *the East to the West*, from Asia to America! And nobly did the Great Russian Church prove herself worthy of the apostolic power of *rightly dividing the Word of Truth* by carrying out the work in all its detail. She faithfully keeps the apostles' will as expressed in these words: *Let the elders that rule well be counted worthy of double honor, especially they who labor in the word and teaching;* she elevates her Missionary to a high post. In his new office as an archpastor, the M. Rev. Innocent created two more dioceses in Eastern Siberia, besides the church of Alaska. He was ever sailing over the ocean, or driving in reindeer and dog sledges over a country thousands of miles in extent, everywhere baptizing the natives, for whom he has introduced the use of letters, and translated the Gospel into their native tongues.

It has been, and still is, the habit of some who are unfriendly to the Orthodox Church to speak of her as a dead church. Such a daring charge could be uttered for three reasons, and they are these: Such persons are either determined upon a certain course of public policy, with no respect for the truth, or they are not inclined to think well of Eastern Christians, whom it would be inconvenient to recognize as brethren while enjoying personal comfort through social connections; but if it be not that, it is then because of a light head and total ignorance of the facts in universal history. In modern times the Russian Church has proved, in more instances than one, that she is alive with the missionary spirit. May we condemn the Slavonic Orthodox Church in the Balkan States, and in Austria, simply because she is struggling for her existence in spite of the aggressive intrusion on her own ground of the brethren of the Society of Jesus? Nor is the influx of American Sectarian preachers in Arabia and in Palestine, a reason which could justify any one in saying that the Church of Christ in those parts is dead! In these days we know something of what enslavement to the Turk involves. And what, in common justice, to say nothing of Christian charity, have we a right to expect from those groaning under such bondage? Have we the conscience to ask that they should make converts, when now for five hundred years they have been struggling, as in a bloody sweat, to keep Christianity alive under Moslem tyranny? And, in that time, how many martyrs of every age and condition have shed a halo around the Oriental Church? Not less than a hundred martyrs of these later days are commemorated in the services of the Church, and countless are the unnamed ones, who have suffered for the faith, in these five hundred years of slavery. In 1821, Gregory, Patriarch of Constantinople, was hung at the door of his cathedral, on Easter Day. Many other prelates and prominent ecclesiastics were put to death in Adrianople, Cyprus, the Ionian Islands, in Anatolia and Mount Athos. And yet, none apostatized from the faith of Christ. Are not such martyrdoms the best way of making converts? It was thus that, in the first three (and more) centuries of our era, the Church was founded in those lands by the apostles and their immediate successors. How can it be said that, among people who could so die for the faith, there was no real spiritual life? Has not the Greek Church shown by her deeds the steadfastness of her faith?

But it is not our purpose to lecture on history. Nor is it that out of mere curiosity we are here. Let us now look to the duty we have before us this hour. We are gathered here to show our gratitude to our benefactor, and also in a becoming way to honor the memory of our dear Archpastor, Metropolitan Innocentius. *Remembering him who has had the rule over us and our fathers*—the Christians of this Diocese; *remembering him who had spoken unto us the Word of God*, let us now, according to the Divine commandment, *consider his end*, so that we may be able the better to follow the example of strong faith, which he gave us throughout his whole life. Although he was much weakened in his last days by old age and sickness, yet the venerable prelate retained his mind clear up to the last, and truly his course on earth was appropriately crowned with a bright Christian end. *Tell them*, he said, as he was about to sleep, *that no eulogies be pronounced at my funeral, they only contain praise. Let them rather preach a sermon, it may be instructive; and here is the text for it: The ways of man are ordered by the Lord.*

SINCERE RELIGION.

WE live in a peculiar age. No time has ever dawned upon the earth like the present era. Startling developments in the world of truth keep the minds of men, to some extent, constantly reaching out after it. More light! greater knowledge! is now the almost universal cry. Great discoveries in science have opened many new and hitherto unknown avenues to the greater physical development of the human family; and at the same time it may be said to be true, that the mental development of man has, to some extent, kept pace. In all this onward movement in the world of material and mental research, men turn to the representative of God among men, and inquire if in the religious world there are any developments; and we find that there are many and great changes in the religious world. Mark you—many and great changes in the world of religious opinion, but very little development in religious life!

Many a searching, although blind, mind has mistaken religion for some philosophical system. Too irreverent and profane handling of religion often makes of it a science, a pastime study. Now and again we come by the way of such who make religion a speculation; yes, and a speculation without a question as to its nature. Do you not know that religion is one of the qualities of your soul? An essential substance, I might say, to be plain, of your self-recognizing, self-satisfied, living spirit? Those who are convinced of this fact are not indifferent to religion. Indifferentism has no place in the serious life of one who seeks to be right-minded.

We hear it frequently remarked that it matters not what one believes if he does right. But if one does not believe right, he does not do the right thing—that is, if his belief is sincere and carried out in practice. If one believes that which is wrong, and still acts otherwise from force of circumstance, he is wrong in heart. A man may believe in polygamy, but the law and common custom may forbid its practice. He would be in outward life aright, but in heart would be a virtual polygamist. And if circumstances were favorable, his life would bear its legitimate fruit. And this is just as true of every other moral evil. It is all-important to believe right. Every false religion which has cursed mankind has started in a wrong belief. It might not have affected practical duties for a time, but the fruit finally developed. Thus belief in that first lie of Satan's (Gen. iii: 4) has borne its legitimate fruit in—first, the deification of the beautiful, and unnatural curiosity; second, self-love, delusion, and idol-worship; third, free-thinking, protesting, infidelity, and anarchy.

Beloved, when I gave all diligence to write unto you of the common salvation, it was needful for me to write unto you, and exhort you that ye should earnestly contend for the faith which was once delivered unto the saints—(Jude, iii). It is worthy, and more, too, it is a duty, to mention the fact that the large number of Bible-worshipers, who daily read the Holy Scriptures, will not see such passages as this. It is strange, yet it is plain to those who understand the human soul. What do those people think of such texts, and also of these: *I will build my church; and the gates of hell shall not prevail against it* (Matt. xvi: 18). *There is one body, and one Spirit, even as ye are called in one hope of your calling. One Lord, one faith, one baptism. One God and Father of all* (Ephesians, iv: 4–6). *And there shall be one fold, and one Shepherd* (John, x: 16). *Therefore, brethren, stand fast, and hold the traditions which ye have been taught, whether by word, or our epistle* (2 Thessal. ii: 15).

To read the Bible does not mean to be a Christian. One may go to church and also study the Holy Scriptures, and yet not be religious. One may be religious, and yet be laboring under false impression, and also untruthful doctrine. If your friend requests you to do something for him, and you, knowing what he said, would still hesitate, had you not been positive of his own opinion of the request. If you are not always positive of a man's idea, even when you have his words, are you sure of God's opinion? Are you so elevated that you can read God's mind?

"Obey and believe in my doctrine," says Rome. "Be free and strive to create a belief for yourselves," say the Sects. But the Church calls to her own, "Let us love one another, that we may with one mind confess Father, Son, and Holy Ghost."

What is the Orthodox Church? This is the thought, which is repeated more than once in the closed closet of the heart; the question silently asked by the inquiring mind; and, beyond doubt, it is a proof of the quickening presence of the "Spirit of Truth, which abideth everywhere," stirring our souls to action superhuman, and to the contemplation of things which are above our comprehension.

Of late, the One Holy Catholic and Apostolic Church is often heard of, and the existence of an Orthodox Catholic Church has come before the notice of the reading masses in Western Europe and America. A grand revelation! And a heavenly blessing is reserved for all religious people who are striving in these latter times to be right-minded.

In the midst of Romanism and Protestantism, free from the fanaticism of a Pius, or the indifferentism of a so-called liberalism, clear of modern congregationalism — almost daily crumbling into isms—we can see a glow, in the midst of this chaos, as if of a new spark created in a combustible mass, which is none other than the light once revealed to Adam, then faithfully preserved in the Church of the old dispensation, and finally intrusted to the *One* and only Church of God—the Alpha and Omega; this spark we now see illuminated to perfection by the new covenant of God with man, the pledge of which is no less than the ETERNAL WORD, the Only-begotten Son of God Himself—the man Jesus, who is the chief cornerstone of the Orthodox Catholic Church, which rests on the foundation of the Apostles, chosen and put into their places by the Supreme Architect—the Lord Jesus Christ. And behold, this is the Holy Orthodox and Universal (Catholic) Apostolic Church—still the ark of salvation for mankind. Could this stronghold, planned by God the Almighty, be obliterated, because of persecution and temptation, and because of the many that willfully stray away, which of themselves break into numerous sects, as the body deprived of life turns to dust? THE GATES OF HELL SHALL NOT PREVAIL AGAINST IT.

We are all obnoxious to error and mistakes,

and it is but natural that we should make due allowance for human weakness and ignorance. If God had left us in our higher concerns to our devices, we should be still groping in the dark like the heathen of old, whom God left to themselves, in order to show how utterly unable the natural man is to find and grasp the supernatural truth. God mercifully revealed to us His truth, and expects us to thankfully accept it, neither doubting nor denying it. Therefore, what in human concerns might be called a liberal concession to our opponents, would in religion be a foul treachery, opposite God's truth intrusted to His Church. It is not liberal, but indifferent, to regard all sorts of religion as equivalent; not to care to what religion one belongs, just as if one was as good or as bad as the other; or, to put it more forcibly, that the claim of one church to teach Christ's truths purely and completely, to the exclusion of all other churches, is not true, and is simply humbug. This is the principle of all worldly people, and it is a fashion to consider a conscientious religious church-life a downright nuisance, though one is still afraid to call it so. The crowd call it liberal not to make any distinction between the teaching of the different churches, just as if truth and untruth could exist one at the side of the other without any disrespect to God, the Author of truth. It is want of faith and conviction, or rather want of taking an interest in religion, that produces this baleful indifference.

It stands to reason that it is sinful to care so little for the revealed truth as to place it on a level with error. You will say, shall we then condemn our erring brethren? By no means. Christ forbids us to judge anybody, for only God knows whether our brother culpably holds the error, or whether he believes it to be the truth. But even if he believes his error to be the truth, error remains error, and never can become truth. Therefore, we must always condemn error, though we may not condemn the person erring, but must pity him that he takes error for truth. If you think it is all the same what a man believes, provided he is convinced that it is the truth, you are mistaken, for the heathen of old, the Jews, the Mohammedans, and the professors of all other religions, believe they possess the truth. Why, then, did God send His only-begotten Son, Jesus Christ, into the world, if mankind could be saved without him? Christ commanded His apostles and their successors to convert the world to Christianity, not to that sort of vague Christianity which we find in the numerous seditions which appropriate this name, but to His one Church, *which is the foundation and pillar of the truth*, and against which the gates of hell can never prevail. He who believes in these words of Christ can never be indifferent to which Church he belongs, nor can he be indifferent whether his friends or acquaintances continue in error. Therefore, it is his first duty never to countenance religious indifference.

Those who will study the doctrine of the Church, not in the errors and weakness of human superstitions and failings, but in her own divinely inspired rites and institutions, will appreciate the matchless purity of our beloved Church. Let us not be misunderstood. We do not assume to ourselves any prerogative of goodness; on the contrary, woe unto us who have so little profited by the perfect holiness of our Mother Church. The best among us fall grievously short of the ideal of the Church, which towers high above us, bearing aloft the standard of the cross.

Truly glorious and divine is the plan of our Church, but beware of judging her by the failures and errors of her unworthy children.

In her daily Liturgy our Mother—the Church—calling the faithful to prayer, teaches us thus: *Let us pray to the Lord for the peace of the whole world, the good estate of the holy churches of God, and the union of them all.*

For the unity of the Faith, and the communion of the Holy Spirit making request, let us commend ourselves and one another and all our life to Christ the God.

SERMON PREACHED IN THE GREEK-RUSSIAN CHURCH, ON ORTHODOX SUNDAY, February 11–23, 1896.

"Behold, this child is set for the fall and rising of many in Israel; and for a sign which shall be spoken against." (*St. Luke*, ii, 34.)

OUR young metropolis of these Pacific shores in the New World is troubled. Some one has aroused the spirit of strife. The minds of thinking people are not at rest. The thoughts of philosophers are caught in a wind of putrid air and blown over the country helter-skelter. The ignorant and vulgar lovers of sensationalism are fired with the fever that heated the brain of the citizens of Ancient Rome when, in the arena, they called: "More men! more beasts! more blood!" And all this in the name of religion; yea, were it in the name only of religion; but scandal is trumped loud and wide in the name not of that mental disease called religion (as a certain person named it a few days ago in the *Morning Call*), but in the name of the religion of the followers of Jesus Christ. When we see the enemy come upon us, we must strengthen our armaments. We need not fear for our fort, though the walls get scraped and there be some that fall over them, as *the gates of hell will not prevail against the Church.* When a serpent has lain its eggs in a fowl's nest, we must cast them out before the simple chicks are devoured. When the wolf is on hand, the shepherd protects all those sheep which he can gather under his care.

While witnessing these unfortunate scenes of contention and discord in which the sacred homes of Christians are assailed, and by which *brother is set up against brother, and neighbor against neighbor,* we are reminded of the words of Simeon the Just: *Behold, this child is set for the fall and rising of many in Israel; and for a sign which shall be spoken against.* The prophetic vision of Simeon is one of the many proofs of the authenticity of the Holy Gospels. And so is the sacred tradition concerning this devout man in harmony with history.

Early history tells us that one of the Ptolemies,—namely, Philadelphus—who came in possession of some of the acquirements of Alexander the Great, and who would have a firmer hold upon the different peoples, studied their different beliefs, and became impressed with the religion of the Jews. Therefore, Philadelphus invited seventy learned scribes in Israel to translate the Holy Scriptures into the official language of his new empire. Holy Tradition tells us that Simeon was one of the seventy; that he was sorely grieved while translating the Prophets, because he could not, in a natural way, understand a passage which he must literally translate, and which was written by the Spirit of God, who is the Lord of both created nature and the laws that sustain nature; furthermore, that *it was revealed unto Simeon, by the Holy Ghost, that he should not see death before he had seen the Lord's Christ.* And when, at the extreme end of a long earthly life, he comes into the temple and *sees the child Jesus, he takes him up in his arms* and utters that sublime farewell of a grateful soul for the merciful Providence of God: *Lord, now lettest thou Thy servant depart in peace, according to Thy Word.*

Yes, the prophecy of this just and devout man has been fulfilled. For *Jesus has been set up for a sign which shall be spoken against.* Do we not see it ourselves, and in a most conspicuous and public manner in this city of San Francisco?

Jesus on the cross, planted again high up on Calvary, that all may see him! Behold, the man! The soldiers who would not tear the cloak of our Saviour, but cast lots for it, are worthy of pity when compared with these dissenters who would rend asunder the Church; yea, the very body of Jesus Christ. Have these destroyers of Faith a mission to fulfill in this world? What is their object in destroying the hope of Christians? Do these boastful humanitarians tell of love? Do they know what is love? Can they give an example or perfect love? What kind of a hereafter do they picture? In what consists their spirituality? Are they not pantheists, with the exception of their masks? What! they deify human kindness? Do they confound the natural *instinct* of kindness (that we see, even in the lower animals,) with love? Christians, do not be discouraged by these jests, but partake of that Divine Love, that complete, perfect love, that eternal, that burning love of Jesus, and pray for your enemies!

Do not think it strange when an Antichrist comes before the great mass of daily newspaper readers and endeavors to undermine their faith in a divine religion. We ought to expect such trials. We must remember that such people are not fundamentally acquainted with the complex make-up of themselves. It may take longer time, if it is necessary, to pick up the separate stones that have been scattered than it did to break down the wall. To deny the Divinity of Jesus Christ and the Gospels, together with the time and character of their authorship, etc., does not prove that a man is learned, not only in theology, but even in profane history. It is useless, and for the majority of mankind it is dangerous, to listen to one talking on the subject of faith, when that one does not himself believe in his own personal spirit, which spirit should be subject to the will of a higher and likewise personal spirit. Faith is not controlled by the worldly. It is an implanted function of the soul, which must be developed, and when faith rightly and freely grows in its spiritual sphere, it is a powerful agent for good to the soul; hence the miracles in the Christian Church.

Again, in our day, *Jesus Christ is set for a sign which shall be spoken against.* Are we, beloved brethren and sisters, prepared to share these calumniations and suffer with our Lord? Are we of those *who will rise again in Israel?* Which are those who belong to the company that is to fall? If we be not of those who are already lying in the bottom of the abyss, and who have never risen, can we flatter ourselves that we are not of those who will, or of those who may, fall? The Word of God, in this instance, does not mention those who have been lying in the depth of condemnation, but those who *will* fall and those who will rise when they step on the stand, face to face, before Jesus Christ?

Beware of self-delusion! Beware of the deceptions of the enemy! Do not think that a man is a real scholar of the Bible because he can quote by memory ever so many passages. Did not the first one who fell from the most elevated condition into the lowest hell, did not Satan know the Word of God? Yea, before it was written into a book by human hand.

Look and see how the Devil quotes from the Bible when he tempted the Lord in the wilderness, and said: *He shall give His angels charge over thee, to keep thee in all thy ways. They shall bear thee up in their hands, lest thou dash thy foot against a stone.* The Devil withheld the words that follow immediately after these, which read: *Thou shalt tread upon the lion and adder; the young lion and the dragon shalt thou trample under foot.*

Now, in these days of comfort, and luxury, and civilization, an affliction is come upon you, O Christians! Now, in these days, when many voluntarily and involuntarily worship the golden calf, you are tempted, O Christians! Now, in these days of enlightenment, when reason is fixed up above all else as a god, set apart from the moving faith of the individual soul, and devoid of the longings of a heart, you are made to feel the abnormal condition of the world you live in, and also to carry a heavier cross for the sake of your weaker brethren, O Christians! Now, in this age of doubt, conflicting claims, and diverse opinions, the eyes of all sincere seekers of the truth are looking toward us who are of the Orthodox religion. Let us attend. Let us stand well, and be true to our great trust! Let us feel our great responsibility, that we may live up to the holy principles of the Orthodox Church of Christ. Let us avail ourselves of this special privilege. Let us profit by the opportunities that this special season affords. I mean this time of fast,—*i. e.* Lent. This is our day of salvation. This is the time for Christian work and prayer. Let us examine ourselves in confession and enrich our experience. Let us renew ourselves in repentance, sanctify ourselves in constant prayer, in order to become worthy of the closest union with our Saviour in partaking of His holy body and precious blood, and thereby live in communion with God. And then, coming into harmony with the all-just, all-wise, all-good Spirit of God, which abides in His Church, no affliction, no persecution, will remove us from the Rock of Salvation, and with a clearer comprehension we will sing with the Church of God: *The Helper and Protector has been unto my salvation; this is my God, and Him will I praise; the God of my father, and Him will I exalt; for he hath been wonderfully glorified. Amen.*

SERMON FOR THE FIFTH SUNDAY AFTER TRINITY.

(*St. Matthew*, viii: 28; ix: 2.)

TO-DAY'S Gospel is a short one, but it contains much instruction for us. The examples and lessons which are to be had from these few words are sufficient to supply those of us who will live the longest with enough thought to last us all our lives. For the present, it is our purpose to point out the most important, that which is for our spiritual good. Here we have offered to us pearls; and it is our duty to invest them in such a manner as to gain a large profit. Our Lord Jesus Christ tells us *not to cast our pearls before the swine, else we ourselves bear the consequences* of our foolishness. Devils are for the swine; rather, the swine are for the devils. But pearls are for Christians. So then, what are these precious pearls we have here offered to us? They are the Word of God, faith and repentance, hope and prayer, love and good works. We must not only behave well, but we must also do good works and love disinterestedly. We must not *merely* hope, but hope *firmly* and *continue in prayer*. We must not have *some* faith, but we must have a *whole* faith, and we must fully *believe*.

I have heard people say that there are no demons or devils. Some of them say that their existence is an abstraction; while others say devils are the wicked people we have about us in the world. We cannot say that such people are unbelievers, for some of them have *some* faith; but it pleases their whim and satisfies their conscience to formulate "their own creed," which suits them, just as his warm bed-cover does the drowsy schoolboy on a wintry morning. Yet there are a few such people who do not believe that there are any personal spirits. But we cannot stop now to discuss the abnormal condition of those opinions, upon which they think they have a foundation for knowledge, and which, at the same time, exclude the possibility of localizing an individuality. In returning to the subject of our remarks, we affirm that, of his own will, the

Devil surely will not reveal himself to people who do not believe; for, should he do so, they might believe, and that would be against his own sly, diabolical policy, as he would have all in the dark, so terrible is his enmity against the Eternal Source of Light and Treasure of Goodness—God Almighty.

Now, for the benefit of those of whom it is said that they have *some* faith (which, by the way, is a logical absurdity): You have the ability of your spiritual faculties; you have the means of grace for your support; you must have a whole faith; you have room for it, if *faith, but only as a mustard-seed, will move a mountain!* Rouse yourselves! The world which you worship only flatters you. The heaviness of your flesh should not keep you back from our Saviour—the God of spirits and of all flesh. If you continue to drowse, you will imperceptibly fall under the influence of the evil spirits, who are anxious for the company even of swine. Be careful that you become not possessed by a devil.

Yes, the two men of the Gadarenes were possessed with devils. They were not common maniacs, nor persons with a disordered function in the cerebral region; for they knew, while the inhabitants of that country did not know, that Jesus Christ was the Son of God. The devils knew that a time was coming when their freedom, which they abused and made such evil use of, would be checked. The devils would not give up the darlings which so readily gratified their passions. It was *torment* for them when the merciful Lord liberated poor mankind. The two unfortunate ones, that were possessed by demons *were exceeding fierce, so that no man could pass by that way.* If the evil spirits torment those whom they possess in such a horrible manner, then what must be the suffering of sinners in hell, where they are bound in company of the devils for all eternity?

Thus it is that some who are supposed to be Christians, and who deceive themselves by thinking that they are believers, while spiritually drowsing console themselves with substitute beliefs, such as superstitious guessings of fortune, communication with the dead, or so-called spiritualistic seances; and there is yet a finer cult, which satisfies the whim of the esthetically inclined; it has an abstract philosophy, and for this reason it is difficult to name it; but nowadays it is often wrongly called *theosophy*. And, again, we see that there are such people, who have no faith whatever, notwithstanding the great number of miracles performed in the Church of Christ, during nearly nineteen centuries. Between Heaven, the habitation of saints, and Hades, or the lower regions, the habitation of the unbelieving sinners, who during their life *have trodden under foot the blood of the Son of God, and have done despite unto the Spirit of Grace* (Heb. x: 26–30), and died in their sins unrepented, there is *fixed* even now *an impassable gulf;* the prayers of the Church, and Christ's unbloody sacrifice of the Altar itself are of no avail for them.

The land of the Gadarenes was a place favored by the legion of darkness. The people disobeyed the law of Moses, if not by using as food the flesh of swine, then by keeping swine for commerce. These people were ungrateful, malicious, and mercenary. When the Lord Jesus Christ delivered the two possessed with devils, and the people lost their herd of *many* swine, they did not think of the sin of breaking the law, nor did they even wonder at the pity shown by the *great Miracle-Worker*, but *they came out*, in a matter of fact way, *and besought Jesus that he would depart from their borders.*

My dear brethren and sisters, let us look to ourselves, that for the appetites of the flesh, the pleasures of frivolous society and false philosophy, and that for gain and business, we lose not Jesus, our Saviour, and fall a prey to the adversary of our eternal salvation. Amen.

SERMON ON THE TWENTIETH SUNDAY AFTER TRINITY.

(*St. Luke*, vii: 2-17.)

IN the three years and several months that Jesus Christ went from town to town, from the hamlets in the hills of Judea to the city of Jerusalem, *not having a place to rest his weary head*, but resting at whatever place offered by the chance of circumstance, without inconveniencing any of His followers or neighbors (do we not find Him asleep in a fisherman's boat?), or feeding on what is offered Him by the love of His disciples or the good women who followed Him in much significant silence and humility, and *preaching the commandment of love*, the *Word of God*, the *Kingdom of Heaven*, doing good *to all sorts of people* that He came in contact with, and helping in one way or another the vast multitude that was so sorely in need of help—and at that, in want of the Only Helper who was able to assist them once and forever in their several strange conditions, and One whom it seems many *waited for*,—He, on one occasion, had just come into the town of Capernaum, when a Roman military officer, whose confidential servant was dying, sent a delegation of *the elders of the Jews, beseeching Jesus that He would come and heal his servant.* Seeing the great faith in this *Gentile*, He would prove it to *the stiff-necked* Jews, for their instruction, because they could not perceive it in its luster of natural simplicity; and so Jesus dismissed them; and *they that were sent, returning to the house, found the servant whole that had been sick.* The Redeemer does not stop here; He stays not to enjoy the praise of the inhabitants of Capernaum. St. Luke tells us, that *on the very next day after, He went into a city called Nain.* The same evangelist tells us that *many of His disciples went with Him, and much people.*

As a weary traveler He goes along the dusty road, seeking another opportunity, going into another city to glorify His Heavenly Father, to benefit His fellow-men, fulfilling His mission of redeeming the world from sin, death, and the Devil.

Now, *when He came nigh to the gate of the city, behold, there was a dead man carried out, the only son of his mother, and she was a widow: and much people of the city were with her. And when the Lord saw her, He had compassion on her, and said unto her, Weep not!* How fortunate for the poor widow that Jesus Christ came nigh to the gate of the city at the very moment when they carried out her dead and only boy! Yes, Jesus Christ is ever ready to be there at the very moment; there, where His consolation is needed; He is always there, where His help is wanted. How many of us are in need of such comforting words! Some among us mourn the loss of dear ones. There are such ones even whose hearts seem to be shriveled to naught from suffering; and it may follow, that they will mourn other losses ere long. But the loving Jesus says, *Weep not!* The power exercised on earth by the God-man was delivered—not stintedly, but gifted freely and wholly—to His Church; and over the expanse of ages this same voice bears the sweet words of comfort to us Christians: *Weep not, for I am the Way and the Life;* and to convince the coarse Jewish multitude, which it seems could never satisfy its sinful hunger for outward signs or miracles appealing to the eyes of flesh, and having compassion on them as well as on the widow, whose only son was dead, *Jesus came and touched the bier: and they that bare the dead stood still. And he said, Young man, I say unto thee, arise!* And by His touch and command the living soul reanimated that form of dead matter, and again housed in its narrow sphere, and I might say, as a holy man had said before, its prison. *And he that was dead sat up, and began to speak. And He delivered him to his mother.* There was something in the serene countenance of this Teacher, who walked with the common people as freely as He could sit with the chief scribes of Judea, a something in the simple country-habited, long-haired Nazarene, who spake great things through one of His glances, so majestic in their silence, that compelled them who bare the dead to stand still. But when the corpse became a living man, *there came a fear on all; and they glorified God, saying, that a great prophet is risen up among us; and, that God hath visited His people.*

Who should glorify God more than we? Was not a great prophet risen, had not Christ himself come, that we should be Christian? Hath not God visited His people that He should abide in us? For now He verily lives in His Church as He once walked with Adam and Eve in Paradise. Yes, beloved Christians, we should be deeply grateful to God for all His works, whether we comprehend them or not, and humble ourselves before the greatness of His glory, and with low and meek hearts pray Him to enlighten our understanding: *Blessed art Thou, O Lord: O teach me Thy justifications.*

When we attentively listen to what is read or sung in the church, then we are the more readily prepared to praise the Lord in a right sense, as the Spirit of God breathes in all the expressions of Christ's Church. Let us illustrate an instance, by recalling to your memory the words you heard here a few weeks ago, at the exaltation of the cross. Let us attend!
" This day, the Master of Creatures, and
" Lord of Glory is nailed to a cross and pierced
" in the side; He, who is the sweetness of the
" Church, tastes gall and vinegar; He, who

"adorns the firmament with clouds, is crowned
"with a wreath of thorns; He, who created
"man, is smitten by a perishable hand; He
"is spit upon; He is buffeted; and he suffers
"all for the sake of me who am condemned,
"my Redeemer and God, that He may save
"the world from seduction, as he is the Merci-
"ful One." Cannot such words of the church-service fill a Christian with *a sorrow that is unto salvation*, with gratitude for the great goodness and wonderful condescension of the Most High, and also with joy for now being able, in a measure, to understand the Supreme Being?

Anything rather than believe in miracles—at the close of the nineteenth century; I, and you yourselves, have heard this saying of the world. The world sees no miracles—it repels, not only the very enthusiasm, but it sometimes is a stumbling-block, even before serene, spiritual reflection — which might work them. " Give a positive sign," the world says, " and I, in spite of new theories, will believe." The answer to such a request was spoken long ago by the Saviour himself: *A faithless and perverse generation asketh for a sign, and no sign shall be given it.*

Where there is no possibility of a miracle of the mind, or of the heart, there is no possibility of a miracle to satisfy the wavering vision of flesh.

Unbelievers often think, or they seem to be anxious to have others think, that they have gained an important point when they wrongly take upon themselves a self-imposed duty of tormenting Christians with such questions as this one: "Why do we not see miracles now?" But if you explain why, which the Christian, with God's help, may do, the unbeliever's reason will not be able to grasp the subject in its entity, and his stone heart will not be moved, as the stiff necks of the Jews did not bend, when, instead of the distinct commands of that imperious, awful voice on the quaking, fiery Mount Sinai, the very Love of God itself came to them, gently knocking at the doors of their hearts—in the person of the crucified Messiah.

For the true Christian, there is no necessity for an answer to this question; he observes, almost daily, the supernatural phenomena working independently and apart from the machinery of the periodical course of natural events, and glorifies *the God that doeth wonders.* The good Christian can be likened unto a candle whose flame burns steadily; but he knows that no one is perfect but God, that he is dependent upon God's grace for steadfastness in the faith, and he does not despair if his flame of light should now and then flutter in the wind of trials and temptations, but he prays to God the more fervently, yea, until, under the heat of battle, the very material of the candle is no more, and his whole existence is offered up to God as a *holocaust.* Furthermore, the orthodox Christian is conscious of the fact that sometimes we do not see miracles, or we see or hear of them rarely, either because they are invisible to us, as unworthy of trust, or because they are not even accomplished, on account of the doubts we sometimes allow to enter our minds. How can the *Word preached to us* work miracles in us, when our heart, like a field wild with tares, is thickly sown with idle words, and overgrown by carnal desires and unlawful thoughts? How can the sacraments work miracles in us, if we approach them but out of absolute necessity, without a careful previous purification, without an ardent aspiration to be united to God? The Apostle Paul, convicting the Corinthians of an unworthy communion of the Body and Blood of Christ, concludes: *For this cause many are weak and sickly among you, and many sleep;* that, is, many are struck with sudden death for insulting holy things. I think that unto some of us it is already a *miracle* of divine mercy if on such occasions we are not visited with similar punishments.

It is not so surprising that the infidel will not perceive the power of God's grace in His Church, as it is, when he will not see the hand of the Creator in all the natural, outward beauty of the universe. Yet the Church, as the Bride of Christ, is unchangeable — as her Lord. The Church shall continue unto the end of time—as liveth her Eternal Head.

He that believeth on me, the works that I do shall he do also; and greater works than these shall he do; said Jesus Christ. And in truth, the deeds of an Elias, a Moses, the works of a Peter, a Paul, and the wonders of a Panteleimon, a Nicholas, are not a strange thing in the Holy Orthodox Church. The like is repeated again and again in the Church, whether you see it or not. You must remember that *the Kingdom of God cometh not with observation.* Some generations after our day the Church on earth may read the records of and treasure the memory of holy lives and mighty deeds accomplished in our day, if not here, then somewhere else, and of which most of us have not the slightest knowledge (?). True miracle-workers do not like to make a show of the miracles. For Jesus Christ Himself, the chief and most perfect type of miracle-workers, who came upon earth that men should know through Him the saving, miracle-working power of God, who, working openly for the sake of divine glory, had no need to guard Himself against the temptations of human glory, possessing against this temptation divine power and glory, and yet seemingly He not so much revealed as hid His miracle-working power.

Now, to return to the words of to-day's Gospel. When we are obliged to bury our loved ones, let us be comforted; *weep not*, says Jesus, for they are not lost to us, for—if they died in communion with the Church—they are still in the fold of Christ. Shall we be selfish and tempt the already boundless mercy of God, which many of us cannot understand, and desire to have all things just to suit ourselves, instead of bowing in submission to the all-wise providence of God? Is it not even now a miracle of divine charity that, being in communion with Christ's Church, and partaking of the same unbloody sacrifice of the body and blood of the Son of God, to which the departed souls look forward, some with anxiety and some with joy, as to an offering on their behalf, an offering most acceptable to the Heavenly Father, that we are in communion with them? And likewise that we shall see again "our fathers and brethren; also the orthodox that lie here and everywhere, who have gone to their rest before us?" For all Thy great mercies and unspeakable love we give thanks to Thee, our God—The Father, the Son, and the Holy Ghost, to whom be all glory, honor, and worship unto the ages of ages. Amen.

HOW THE CHURCH CARES FOR HER SHEEP AND LAMBS.

"I will pour my spirit upon thy seed, and my blessing upon thine offspring; and they shall spring up as among the grass, as willows by the water-courses. One shall say, I am the Lord's, and another shall subscribe with his hand unto the Lord." (*Isaiah*, xliv: 3, 4, 5.)

WE often hear the Church spoken of as our Mother. I will now explain to you in what way and for what reason the Church truly is our Mother. All of us Christians have two births: one is according to the flesh, of nature; the other is spiritual, when a person receives the Grace of God, and through baptism becomes a member of the Church. Therefore, the Church, by right of spiritual birth, becomes our Mother; then, again, she is entitled to that right by the religious instructions which she offers to us; she also enjoys the full right of motherhood, by virtue of the care she has for us, and of the Providence with which she is gifted for our salvation. *Can a woman forget her sucking child, that she* should not have compassion on the son of her womb? Yea, they may forget, yet will I not forget thee. Behold, I have graven thee upon the palms of my hands; thy walls are continually before me. (Isaiah, xlix, 15, 16.) With these words, the Prophet of old comforted the people, who bitterly complained of their condition, as they needed the Grace of God, and waited the Saviour, who was to give it to them. And now, thanks to that love of God, which we cannot describe with our human tongues, we live in the good age of opportunities; *the Grace of God has touched us; yea, the Son of God walks in the midst of men.*

Yet the Grace of God is not like the air, which is poured out alike for all nature and all mankind; the merits of the suffering and death of Jesus Christ on the cross are not appropriated to men *against their will.* The virtue of our Lord's glorification does not sanctify every one of us alike; His Apostle says: *There is one glory of the sun, and another glory of the moon, and another glory of the stars: for one star differeth from another star in glory. So also is the resurrection of the dead.* (1 Cor. xv: 41-42.)

Jesus, who gave Himself as a price for to redeem man from the Devil, from the sufferings of sins, from spiritual and therefore eternal death, He, our Saviour, demands, that we be faithful followers of His word, in order to retain the new life while we yet walk in the dangerous path of this material world, while we yet may fall a prey to the changes of time. Jesus Christ, our Lord and God, will, at the last terrible Judgment Day, exact of us who call ourselves Christians an account as to how we have fulfilled His commandments. *I will build my Church*, He said; and we who have the privilege of being members of His organization, must be obedient and keep within the bounds, for He has fixed a limit, as well as He has beautifully reared the whole of parts. He, the anxious shepherd of His flock, has also said: *If thy brother neglect to hear the Church, let him be to thee as an heathen man and a publican.* (Matt. xviii: 17.) Likewise, the faithful servant of Jesus Christ, St. Paul, who jealously guarded the purity and wholesomeness of the Church, has said: *For there are unruly ones, vain talkers and deceivers, whose mouths must be stopped; who subvert whole houses, teaching things which they ought not, for filthy lucre's sake.* (Tit. i: 10, 11.)

Now, I think, the object of to-day's lesson can be explained more clearly for you; *i. e.* that the Church is our Mother, and that we ought, with stronger faith, give up ourselves to her care, earnestly studying her services and law, and the measures of discipline by which she seeks to benefit all of us in this earthly life, as well as to prepare us for our everlasting home. Time and again you have been told from this holy altar how the Holy Church, our Mother, besides giving spiritual birth to her children, and confirming them in moral strength by the Holy Ghost, then feeding them with the body and blood of the Lamb of God; how, besides this, she guides them in all those things which are necessary in every-day home-life, and likewise for the prosperity of sober and honorable citizens.

The true Christian asks the Church to extend her blessings over his fields, his cattle, his vineyard, his fishing-boat, and over the material and place where he intends to build a home or a house of business, that he may be reminded that Christian laws are to rule the establishment where a Christian earns his living; likewise his sleeping and cooking apartments. Parents ask the Church to invoke God's blessing over the heads of their young children who are just commencing their school-days; and public thanks are offered up when young people have successfully graduated. When the inhabitants of a province or state celebrate the anniversary of some noble patriot, or when, in general, Christians commemorate the virtues of a holy man, a hero of the Cross, their holiday (feasting and innocent merry-making) is crowned with the prayer and blessing of the Church of which the saint himself is still an active member! The sick are brought before the altar where the Church of Jesus Christ assembles; prayers are asked for those who are making voyages by sea or land, and the poor are remembered. Commending ourselves, and one another, the beatings of many hearts are heard in the one voice of our Mother, the Church, when she offers her prayers, together with the saints, for the weak members of the body who are given to sinful passions, and for those who, by their sacrilegious stubbornness, have fallen from the Grace of God! Yes, the Church is the only school where man may learn how to grow to the full measure of true manhood, *unto the measure of the growth of Christ.* Should we not then give more attention to the little children in our congregation? Ah, yes! This is an obligation required of all Christians. The Church is particularly anxious concerning the welfare of children. The responsibility of parents for their children is very great. They are, in fact, the earthly guardians in custody of the children of Almighty God, their Heavenly Father. Teach the little ones. Yet before their minds are capable of retaining impressions — speak to their hearts, mould them to the form of the beautiful and holy. Make over them the sign of the life-giving Cross. Teach them to distinguish from other pictures a painting of our good Lord, or His Holy Mother, and some Biblical sketch. At first, the child may not know, but it can easily be made to feel that God always sees it, when it is naughty, etc. While He was on earth, working out for us our salvation, the Son of God said: *Suffer the little children to come unto* me, for of such is the Kingdom of God. (Luke, xviii: 16.) *Take heed that ye despise not one of these little ones; for I say unto you that in heaven their angels do always behold the face of My Father which is in Heaven.* The teaching of the Gospel plainly tells us that the children of the Select have their angels in heaven, which —as their representatives—can rejoice on their account, as well as they can become offended for any wrong done to them. When it becomes possible for you to teach your little children to pray together with the angels, then you will experience a better change in the moral and spiritual condition of your family.

Ah, yes! Parents are ever anxious over their children! They give much of their strength, of their time, and of their money in order to make of their children mechanics, merchants, laborers, artists. Some — but not many — add to this their patriotic zeal, so as to give to their country good citizens. This is necessary, and very good. But do we not also see around us great abuse in the education and bringing up of children? We now and then see children, dressed in fine and soft clothing, who do not know how to greet a friend, or who have no consideration whatever for an old person.

Yes, luxury has harmed many a son and cursed the life of many a daughter. If you are Christians, then give your children, above all, a Christian education. Many books and papers are now printed which sell for little money. Do not allow them to select their own reading. The food for their minds must be given with great discrimination, else they develop passions, false characters, and, with their poisoned minds, create disturbances in society. Does it not make you feel happy when any one praises you, or your children, and exclaims, "What a clever person! What a beautiful person!" This happiness is not enough for the Church. She strives to give us a higher name; she strives to instruct her children so, that when each one of them is looked upon, one who cannot read will be able to read in their faces and actions their holy name: *A man of God, a noble Christian woman!* And those which do not shine with the light of God's life within them are not Christians at heart.

"Ah! I do not think," says St. John

Chrysostom, "that there are many among the priests which will be saved. I think, rather, there are many more among them which will be condemned!" Therefore, the holy Church, which is also anxious for her ministers, requires the aid of parents in giving their children a wholesome Christian education. Especially the sponsors—*i. e.* the godfather and godmother—are responsible for the moral and religious welfare of their children according to the Spirit. Living together in the Church of God, with all the opportunities before us to-day, let us hope that the words of the holy prophet will be fulfilled for us also: *I will pour my spirit upon thy seed, and my blessing upon thine offspring; and they shall spring up as among the grass, as willows by the water-courses. One shall say, I am the Lord's, and another shall subscribe with his hand unto the Lord.* Amen.

www.ingramcontent.com/pod-product-compliance
Lightning Source LLC
Chambersburg PA
CBHW031831230426
43669CB00009B/1306